NORDIC NARRATIVES OF THE SECOND WORLD WAR

Nordic Narratives of the Second World War

National Historiographies Revisited

Henrik Stenius, Mirja Österberg
&
Johan Östling (eds.)

NORDIC ACADEMIC PRESS

Nordic Academic Press
P.O. Box 1206
SE-221 05 Lund, Sweden
info@nordicacademicpress.com
www.nordicacademicpress.com

Typesetting: Frederic Täckström www.sbmolle.com
Cover: Jacob Wiberg
Cover image: Scene from the Danish movie
Flammen & Citronen, 2008. Nimbus film/Tonny Madsen, Denmark.
Print: ScandBook AB, Falun 2011
ISBN: 978-91-85509-49-2

Contents

Preface

The first step towards writing this book on the Nordic narratives of the Second World War was taken at a seminar hosted by the Norden Institute in Finland (Nifin) in Helsinki on 27 November 2007. The seminar, entitled 'Nordiska en-doktrinstater: nya och gamla analyser av de nordiska staterna under andra världskriget', was opened by Henrik Stenius at the Centre for Nordic Studies at University of Helsinki (CENS), that has been the driving force institution behind this book project. Presentations at the seminar were given by Henrik Meinander (University of Helsinki), Lars Mjøset (University of Oslo), Uffe Østergård (Copenhagen Business School) and Johan Östling (Lund University). At the next stage, the network was extended with Synne Corell (University of Oslo), Guðmundur Hálfdanarson (University of Iceland) and Bo Stråth (University of Helsinki). Mirja Österberg (CENS) was appointed coordinator of the network.

The Joint Committee for Nordic Research Council for the Humanities and the Social Sciences (NOS-HS), a research funding body under the Nordic Council of Ministers, has financially supported the network that put together this volume. Thanks to their funding, we were able to arrange two subsequent meetings, the first in Copenhagen and the second in Lund.

The making of this anthology has had an element of unpremeditation, space for intellectual creativity, questioning and revaluations. Contrasting national narratives and revisions of these interpretations with one another offered insights that forced the writers of this volume to react to new questions and new perspectives, and to think new thoughts.

On behalf of the whole network group, the editors would like to express their gratitude to Nifin, CENS, NOS-HS and Nordic Academic Press, and to Pirkko Hautamäki, who helped us beyond measure by checking our English.

Helsinki and Lund

Henrik Stenius, Mirja Österberg & Johan Östling

CHAPTER I

Nordic Narratives of the Second World War

An Introduction

More than seventy years since the outbreak of the Second World War, the great catastrophe still rumbles on. Indeed, the battle over the meaning of the conflict rages, not least in Europe. In recent decades, the legacy of the war has sparked inflamed debates on how to interpret the past across the Continent. In France and Belgium, heated discussions about collaborators and resistance fighters broke out in the 1980s, and in Austria and Italy a tardy examination of the history of the war years slowly began. The end of the Cold War, moreover, brought forgotten memories and suppressed experiences back to life. In neutral countries, appeasement, foreign policy and financial relationships with Nazi Germany have been a recurrent theme of debate since the early 1990s. Also in many parts of Eastern and Central Europe – from Kragujevac in Yugoslavia to Jedwabne in Poland – the Second World War has entered the public discourse. What was common to all the debates was a pungent smell of hypocrisy, as if Europeans had been living with a misguided history of the war.[1]

Today, at some distance from the most hot-tempered contentions of the war, a general pattern has emerged: the debates were all confrontations between old and new narratives of the Second World War. Although they had much in common, the controversies were at the same time shaped by national traditions and experiences. To grasp fully the character and dynamics of the transformation of these interpretations, it is necessary to focus on a limited number of national contexts.

In this book, these national contexts are comprised of the five Nordic states. While the political cultures in Denmark, Finland, Iceland, Norway and Sweden have their own important specificities, these countries developed a similar social and economic system in the course of the twentieth century. In terms of security policies and their trajectories of the Second World War, however, the Nordic states differ rather dramatically. Denmark and Norway were occupied by Germany, and Iceland by Britain and the United States. Many Finns suffered badly in 1939–1945 in repeated military operations first with the Soviet Union and then with German troops, whereas the Swedes, by contrast, were spared atrocities, desolation and loss of life. Not surprisingly, the Nordic countries have had differing canonised narratives of the Second World War, and the revisions of these patriotic narratives have differed accordingly.

Working on Nordic narratives of the Second World War, putting together the network's goals and outlines for this anthology, writing and disseminating the individual chapters, and last but not least, composing the introductory chapter, has been an interesting challenge with many twists and turns. New questions have arisen while we have attempted to put the war experiences in new perspectives. It has become clear that during the whole process there have been four distinctive tensions that the network has grappled with. The five national analyses of how the narratives of involvement in the Second World War have been fashioned and revised over time show that they all bring to the fore the following tensions:

Security policy doctrines. There is a tension between security policy doctrines and interpretations of the Nordic countries' involvement in the war. It is obvious that history writing as a political activity has depended on the security arrangements the writer is living with.

Democratisation of foreign policy. Who has the right to take part in foreign policy debates and deliberations? To what extent have security policy issues been regarded as an exclusive policy area for the political elite, and to what extent are security arrangements an issue for the general public?

Moral turn. In what sense did the end of the Cold War cause changes – leading to a 'moral turn' – in the way the Nordic countries' involvement in the Second World War has been evaluated? Can one identify new moral dimensions in the interpretations compared with those prevailing during the Cold War? What has the role of the Holocaust been in the five Nordic countries?

Lack of Nordic similarities. One can question whether there are any signal similarities in the narratives of the Second World War in the five Nordic countries. Nordic citizens look upon the world in many important respects in a similar way, which could be called 'Nordic'. But in the field of security arrangements views have been too divergent to amount to decisive common patterns. In the end, one could argue that if one wants to look for similarities, one had best focus on only three of the Nordic countries, that is, Denmark, Norway and Sweden, and conclude that these three countries have one fundamental experience in common: the trauma of not providing a forceful defence or indeed not contributing to the defeat of Nazism. Finland and Iceland have not been much haunted by such considerations.

This introduction will address these tensions by underlining that one can look at these issues from different perspectives, not by casting about for one single truth.

The Patriotic Narrative

The divergences between older and newer interpretations of the Second World War have developed into a specific and vital field of research. Of course, such studies differ in their empiric and theoretical approaches, but they share an interest in the Second World War as constituting the national self-understanding and historical consciousness in European countries throughout the post-war era.[2] All seek to explore the tension between the experience of the second half of the twentieth century and the memory of the first. 'This sharp contrast often seems mind boggling – it runs through individual life experiences as much as through the collective history of the age,' as the historians Konrad H. Jarausch and Michael Geyer have put it.[3]

Moreover, the nature and change of academic historiography is closely connected with the transformation of the greater history culture. Throughout Europe, heated public controversies broke out in the 1980s and 1990s around issues related to the Second World War, from the *Historikerstreit* in West Germany to the debates on the Vichy regime in France, *la Resistenza* in Italy and Kurt Waldheim in Austria. Suddenly the legacy of the war years turned out to be a rich source for political and moral discussions, a challenging question for politicians, intellectuals and historians.

In the course of the 1990s, many historians took part in the national controversies, not least by analysing the formation of a patriotic memory following the end of the war. In his study of Belgium, France and the Netherlands, for instance, Pieter Lagrou stressed the importance of the glorification of the resistance movement, which resulted in the experiences of those who did not fit into the national narrative – Jews, Communists, collaborators – being suppressed and neglected. The memory of the war was nationalised. Only after several decades, when the reconstruction and integration of post-war society was accomplished, could the monolithic memory slowly dissolve and give way to new interpretations of the Second World War.[4] In a similar way, Claus Bryld and Anette Warring examine how a hegemonic narrative of the German occupation of Denmark in 1940–1945 emerged in the immediate post-war years. In its character, this 'basic narrative of the occupation' (*grundfortælling om besættelsestiden*) was markedly nationalistic. A leading principle was that the Danes had fully supported the resistance. Of course, a distinction could be made between active and passive opposition, but with the exception of a few traitors, the entire Danish populace had joined in the struggle against the foreign invaders. Under the influence of the approaching Cold War, the narrative gradually took a more mythical shape: good versus evil, democracy versus dictatorship, universalism versus racism. This national interpretation dominated textbooks, television programmes and historical jubilees during the entire post-war period, underpinning Danish national identity.[5] As Uffe Østergård underlines in his chapter in this volume, however, professional historical research renders the picture both more nuanced and complex.

The various national narratives that Lagrou, Bryld, Warring and others reveal have many features in common: France, Belgium and the Netherlands shared to a large extent Denmark's destiny during and after the Second World War. But many other European countries had utterly different experiences. For some, the war brought a human and material obliteration without precedent; for others, the destruction was almost non-existent. In some countries public morale was strengthened by the war, as the citizens felt they had a part in defeating Nazi rule. A few neutral countries did not take part in the war itself, but were still profoundly affected.[6]

Despite such diversity, almost all national narratives of the Second World War fit into a larger European pattern. The Franco-German historian Etienne François has identified the common elements in this historical landscape. Fundamental, both in the liberal democracies in Western Europe and the Communist dictatorships in Eastern Europe, was the victory over Nazi Germany. The descriptions of the end of the war and of the Liberation often highlighted national unity. The newly won liberty opened a door to the future and marked the beginning of a bright new chapter in history. A common characteristic in most national narratives was also the glorification of the resistance movement, while in countries that had been liberated by foreign troops, domestic efforts tended to be highly esteemed. In addition, the heroisation of the war was another common denominator in the narratives: the heroes included not only charismatic victors such as Charles de Gaulle, Winston Churchill and Josip Broz Tito, but also brave partisans and members of the resistance.[7]

Etienne François has characterised the national narratives of the Second World War in the first decades after 1945 as *patriotic*. This is perhaps a somewhat misleading notion, since the narratives were not permeated with chauvinistic rhetoric or even love of country. 'Patriotic', however, refers to the mere fact that the narratives in this period aimed to adjust the interpretations to the existence of a common national interest. In the patriotic interpretation, victory over Nazism could essentially be ascribed to national achievements, whether the resistance movement, superiority in forces or a more advanced social system. The view was nationally dictated, and the arguments drew their force from a self-righteous ethos. The war years had meant hardship and suffering, but thanks to ideals and virtues, the country gained strength and managed to subdue the aggressive invading power. In countries which had had strong Nazi or Fascist organisations, such as Germany, Austria and Italy, these currents in political culture were often regarded as foreign elements, as alien powers that had taken control of their own people.[8]

Without neglecting the important differences between Eastern and Western Europe, the great majority of the national narratives of the Second World War were united in a patriotism which justified the present pattern of society and vindicated the dominant ideological viewpoint. In many countries, the war had demolished the social community and diluted human trust. The Manichaean heroism of the patriotic narratives offered a remedy, not least in re-establishing the credentials of the nation-state, which had proved disastrously incompetent in protecting the lives of its citizens during the war.[9] The historian Tony Judt has argued that Europeans had a complicated balancing act in having to revitalise the Continent economically and politically by holding the near past back, whereas cultural and moral invigoration at the same time required that they learned from this very past.[10]

In conclusion, the post-war national narratives of the Second World War were modelled on similar prototypes. Firstly, the patriotic interpretation helped to legitimise certain values. In Western European democracies, where anti-totalitarianism became an ideological prop during the Cold War, political opponents were successfully stigmatised. In Eastern Europe, by contrast, anti-Fascism was at the core of the patriotic staging. Secondly, the capacity to defend and mobilise the nation was the very hub of all narratives. The resistance could draw its strength from personal, national or ideological convictions, but in the end the mutual struggle had benefited the public good, whether the general aspiration was Communism, democracy or peace. Finally, as official patriotic narratives, they were all narrated within a national framework, not necessarily expressing a nationalistic understanding, but certainly operating with the help of a 'methodological nationalism'.[11] They could of course be part of a wider international context, but the nation-state was the origin and the goal of patriotism. As a consequence, the Holocaust was not regarded as a central element in the narratives of the Second World War, particularly since a large number of the victims, Jews as well as Roma, lacked a nation-state of their own.[12]

At the centre of many of the academic studies in the 1990s was the deconstruction or contextualising of the patriotic narratives of the Second World War. A common conclusion was that every country in Europe seemed to have developed its own 'Vichy syndrome', to use the expression that Henry Rousso coined in his pioneering work on the French failure to come to terms with what had happened during the war and the desire to recast the memory to fit into a post-war national narrative.[13] By challenging official history writing and the interpretation of the resistance movement, a new national understanding of the war began to emerge, at least in many parts of Western Europe.

The Holocaust and European Universalism

Step by step, the patriotic narratives lost their influence in Europe, as the understanding of the war increasingly became part of a shared European experience. What was new was the theme of the Holocaust and European universalism that were brought to the centre of the interpretations of the Second World War. This change was clearly linked to the end of the Cold War. The patriotic narratives, which had partly been constructed in order to unite the nation and also to legitimate the post-war politics of the nation-state during the Cold War, were no longer needed for the purpose they had been constructed for. This change enabled both a new moral turn in interpretations of the Second World War and a democratisation of foreign policy.

Former monolithic narratives were challenged; new or previously suppressed interpretations gained ground. In the Federal Republic of Germany, which was in many ways an exception as the successor of Nazi Germany, a new attitude about the past was perceived in the early 1960s, but the German lessons remained exclusively German and strengthened rather than softened the self-righteous tone in other parts of Europe. German *Vergangenheitsbewältigung* (the process of coming to terms with the past) probably had the effect that the Nazis continued to be seen as primarily a German problem, while other European countries could remain onlookers. More profound national confrontations were hence delayed.[14] However, in the Nordic case, the European framing was of a particular, enduringly parochial kind. The exceptions were notable but few. Nordic scholars have not contributed original, robust interpretations of the events of the Second World War internationally. What was new was only a contextualisation of national experience in a European perspective. The Nordic analysts remained reticent on, for instance, Roosevelt's collaboration with the Vichy regime, the liberation/occupation of the Baltic states by the Red Army at the end of the war, or on the necessity of the bombing of Dresden. It is in this particular sense that the Nordic analysts and commentators were not 'European' and still remain so.

However, as a general rule the leitmotifs of the national narratives of the Second World War have undergone a fundamental change in the last decades, shifting from *patriotism* to *universalism*, or at least shifting from outright methodological nationalism. If heroic deeds and brave resistance were in the forefront of the interpretations until the 1980s or even later, the new universalistic narratives depart from grievous, traumatic experiences. Without parallel, the Holocaust became the starting-point in this universalistic staging of the European narratives. The extermination of the European Jews was known about even during the war, but it was not until the very end of the twentieth century that the Holocaust emerged as the predominant moral lesson of the Second World War. In a world that had experienced Stalinism, Fascism and imperialism, the Holocaust marked a dark century's deepest abyss.[15]

At the same time, victims gained prominence in the public sphere, and many of history's malefactors were brought to trial decades after the end of the war. The Eichmann trial in Jerusalem in 1961 and the Auschwitz trial in Frankfurt in 1963–1965 anticipated the legal proceedings in the 1980s and 1990s. Furthermore, companies, banks and states were forced to repay illegal profits made in the 1930s and 1940s. An additional component in the new attitude toward the Second World War was the rise of an official culture of grief and commemoration, not least paying tribute to the memory of the murdered Jews. With monuments, exhibitions and memorial days, the Second World War in general and the Holocaust in particular were brought to the centre of public attention. States, organisations and individuals took the blame upon themselves for crimes committed during the war. The Stockholm International Forum on the Holocaust in 2000 marked a turning-point for this new, universalistic narrative.[16] The Swedish Prime Minister Göran Persson set the tone by stating that Sweden had now 'entered the world of the high politics of morality'.[17] Whereas Sweden, Denmark and Norway have been members of the Task Force for International Cooperation on Holocaust Education, Remembrance and Research since 2004, Finland first became a full member in December 2010.[18]

This major shift in the interpretations of the Second World War must also be related to general tendencies in contemporary scholarly and intellectual debate. Firstly, recent decades have in many ways seen the return of history. The historian Pierre Nora has talked about the 1990s as 'l'ère de la commémoration' for Europe, as a period when experiences and recollections of the war years came back. After the linguistic and cultural turns in academic scholarship, historians, ethnologists, sociologists and others have devoted much energy to studying representations of the past and manifestations of public memory.[19]

Secondly, the historian George Cotkin has spoken of history's 'moral turn' in recent years. 'Armed with social scientific objectivity and methods', he writes, 'historians since the late nineteenth-century have generally eschewed the language of morals.' At the same time, however, they constantly confront ethical and ideological questions in their work, tending to 'write moral tales, albeit more or less consciously'. According to Cotkin, a heightened interest in the relationship between history and morality was discernible in the 1980s and early 1990s, and accelerated after the Cold War and the genocidal bloodletting in Bosnia and Rwanda. Since then, quite a few historians and philosophers have written on various aspects of the Second World War from an ethical point of view, including Jonathan Glover, Anthony Grayling and Michael Bess. In general, the numerous studies on human rights, war crimes and the Holocaust testify to a 'moral turn' in contemporary historiography.[20]

It is obvious that this is not the last paradigmatic shift concerning the interpretation of the Second World War. Although it is difficult to predict what future will hold, Norman Davies has suggested that whereas the Second World War has mainly been interpreted in 'Americocentric' terms since the 1990s, as a consequence of the fact that the United States was the sole superpower that emerged after the Cold War, this view will eventually be challenged by new interpretations when new superpowers appear.[21]

Moral Turn, Pluralism and Democratisation

In studying the Nordic indications of a 'moral turn' – and in particular the way scholars have rejected the traditional, patriotic narratives of the Second World War – one has to relate the paradigm shift to the breakthrough of new debating patterns and decision-making procedures on security issues at large that was to a certain extent a consequence of the end of the Cold War. In its essence, the novelty consisted of the simple fact that there was no longer just *one* justifiable security policy arrangement, but several. During the Cold War, the one-doctrine axiom was particularly firmly rooted in all the Nordic countries. In Sweden, the preferred term was 'small-state realism' – which Johan Östling discusses in his chapter – based on the assumption that there are no foreign policy alternatives for small states and there are therefore no moral considerations, other than to keep the one and only security policy doctrine, a moral obligation that can be seen as both moralistic and idealistic. However, fascinatingly, in a comparative Nordic perspective, one should note that each Nordic country chose its own foreign policy doctrine. In addition, each of these national security arrangements was regarded as invalid in neighbouring Nordic countries, although there was a strong resemblance between the Danish and Norwegian foreign policy thinking. By the end of the Cold War, it became difficult to uphold a consensus on foreign policy and security arrangements, as there was no longer a commonly accepted enemy. Only the alternative, the possibility to choose between several foreign policy alternatives, makes talk of a 'moral' turn relevant.

The new situation, with its complex pattern of threats, implied, firstly, a contestation of the idea that a small nation can or should have only one security policy at a time (although the powers that be always seek to give the impression that the nation unanimously stands behind the official, indivisible security policy doctrine). Secondly, the new situation implied that foreign policy had been democratised. One argument in this anthology is thus that the single foreign policy strategy was abandoned, while the citizenry became legitimate participants in foreign policy deliberations.

Take the post-1990s change in Finnish foreign policy debate, which relates to the argument Dag Anckar made already in 1984 that Finland's foreign policy may have moved in a more democratic direction after the 1982 presidential election. This would have implied replacing *realism* with *morals*. The increased interest in foreign policy in the Finnish mass media, spiced with more than a hint of commercialism and sensationalism, made it impossible to control the debate. Generally speaking, increased information on foreign policy gives voters different alternatives, which in turn increases their engagement in foreign political issues, and ultimately takes foreign policy from being an exclusive, elite-dominated matter to one among many.[22] For Sweden's part, Kjell Goldmann has detected an analogous shift in the 1980s. Swedish foreign policy became 'politicised' in the sense that political parties articulated their own foreign policy positions, although Goldmann does not view the shift as an unequivocal or dramatic change, but rather as a slow evolution.[23] Nevertheless, although we have to wait until the 1980s to see a public debate with explicit demarcations, the shift seems to have found official consent in Finnish governmental documents even later. For instance, a report by the Foreign Ministry of 2001 registered that the ministry had traditionally been kept at a distance from the general public, but that this was now changing. Foreign policy was becoming a topic like any other on the public agenda.[24] Therefore it seems that there was a kind of democratisation of foreign policy: unlike previously, the Nordic countries' populations were now invited to deliberate on foreign policy matters.

The right to take part in foreign policy debates has been rigidly restricted in all parts of the world at all times. In the Nordic case its history can be characterised as an exceptionally smooth move from *approval* to *deliberation.* However, some paradigmatic stepping stones in this move are worth noting. Firstly, one can notice that in times of strong republican policies, the right to engage in foreign policy was limited. A striking example comes from the history of Sweden in the so-called Age of Liberty in the mid eighteenth century, when the Diet had an extraordinary influence on the politics of the reign, and the peasantry, too, constituted a political Estate. Even so, there were restrictions stating that the peasant Estate did not have the right to decide on matters of foreign policy, while they did have the right and the duty to decide on all other matters on the Diet's agenda.

Secondly, a smooth change took place in the nation-building period after the French Revolution, as the people, largely conceptualised as the peasantry, were politically upgraded to the legitimate driving force of the nation. The new ideology of a nation-state could no longer be sanctioned solely by dynastic arguments. The practical implications of this new way of legitimising political power were that the people/peasantry were invited to commit themselves to foreign policy in a very particular mode. Social and political mass mobilisation as popular movements led the peasantry to take a public stand on foreign policy issues, but only when their approval was sought for various patriotic campaigns the political elite were keen for them to join. A case in point is the fundraising campaign for submarines in Sweden in 1912. In the Norwegian history of the nineteenth century, there was a unique case when the commoners, mostly the peasantry, were given an opportunity not only to approve the political elite's preferred foreign policy doctrine, but also publicly and ostentatiously to choose between two different foreign policies. This occurred in the 1870s and 1880s, when both the conservatives and the liberals in Norway mobilised the public into their own separate, voluntary rifle guards. Popular approval of an officially authorised foreign policy through engagement in voluntary civil guards became exceptionally important in Finland too, not only during the civil war of 1918, but also in the 1920s and 1930s, when powerful elements in the Finnish political elite felt that voluntary mobilisation should shoulder much of the responsibility of military preparedness. After the Second World

War, and during the Cold War in particular, the general public were once again asked for their approval, but now of a different kind, when there were public exhibitions of friendship with the Soviet Union in the media and in voluntary associations.

Asking for approval is thus part of a centuries-long tradition in the consensual and inclusive history of the Nordic countries. However, this show of humility has changed in recent decades as the security arrangement policies became more and more dependent on public opinion. One might argue that in a long historical perspective, the debate in the 1990s on Finland joining NATO stands out as illustrating the paradigm shift. Since the 1990s, the Finnish political elite has been in favour of membership of NATO. However, polls show that the majority of Finns do not support this course of action. Pushing such a security-policy solution has therefore been regarded unthinkable as long as a clear majority of the population is against membership.

Similarities and Dissimilarities

As the chapters in this book will show, the traditional patriotic narratives of the Second World War met with the discourse of a moral turn in a way that varied according to Nordic country in question. What then were the crucial similarities and differences in the way history writing in the Nordic countries constructed traditional patriotic narratives, and how did it come to re-evaluate the established interpretations of the countries' engagement in the Second World War?

The first cluster of questions deals with the content and form of the narratives as well as the position they have had in the general master narratives of the nation. One has to start with the fundamental reality that the patriotic narratives in the Nordic countries were constructed differently, because the fundamental experiences of the war varied from one country to another: the Danes gave up control of their territory without resistance; Norway was occupied despite resistance; Iceland, situated outside the main theatre of operations, was occupied. The Finns succeeded in defending their territory or most of it, thanks to their own military action and their joint efforts with the German military forces; the Swedes officially stood outside the war. This is a theme Bo Stråth elaborates on in his contribution to this volume.

The Nordic experiences made up a European microcosm, although none of the Nordic countries could really boast to of being one of the winning countries. Nor were they apprehended by themselves or by others as being on the losing side. Two of the Nordic countries belonged to the small group of non-occupied European nations, while three were part of the much larger group under occupation, but not one of them shared the Eastern European experience of occupation first from the west and then from the east. These fundamental differences meant that the history writing in Denmark and Norway (but not in Iceland) frames it in terms of resistance, expressing it with the help of a *rhetoric of resistance*, whereas Finland and Sweden were focused on defence and the *rhetoric of defence* and *military preparedness*.

One should also ask how experience matches the general master narratives of the Nordic nations. Are they integral or just parenthetical? In the national master narratives of Denmark, Norway and Finland, the experiences of the war have a predominant position, although their nature varies, whereas the war is more peripheral in the Icelandic and Swedish understanding of their national history. In fact, in his contribution, Guðmundur Hálfdánarson shows that the Second World War does not have any distinctive place in Icelandic history writing. This is remarkable considering that the years 1939–1945 were marked by a radical erosion of the geopolitical isolation of Iceland and saw the completion of full statehood after twenty-six years of dual monarchy with Denmark. Firstly, says Hálfdánarson, in the absence of the problem of Nazi collaborators, the memory of the war did not involve moral controversies. Secondly, the war did not fit into the grand narratives of the Icelandic history which had as an unquestioned point of departure the notion that the consolidation of an independent Icelandic nation was first and foremost monitored by the Icelandic people themselves (and was not a result of geopolitical momentum).

History writing in Denmark and Iceland nevertheless shows that conceiving of the war as an episode in parentheses can mean different things. The narrative of the German occupation of Denmark has taken pole position in the Danish understanding of history. However, in the long-term analysis of the political and societal development of Denmark, the period of occupation is comprehended as a parenthesis without any deeper impact on Danish society. History writing in Iceland indicates a diametrically opposite way of positioning the war in national history. That Icelandic society underwent strikingly dramatic changes during the Second World War is acknowledged, but the war itself does not have a particularly pronounced place either in old or new national narratives.

Compared to the Danish and Icelandic positioning, Finnish and Norwegian history writing lends this period a very different importance. In the history writing of both countries, the Second World War has a crucially central position in society, both among professional and popular historians, as is shown by Henrik Meinander's and Synne Corell's contributions to this volume. In Finland, all history writing, regardless of the level or section of society in focus, underlines the significance of the Second World War and its extraordinary and dramatic experiences, whether examining the elites of society or the conditions of everyday life. The impact of the war is recognised on every level. Norwegian history writing acknowledges a similarly decisive impact of war experiences on the master narratives of Norway, almost unavoidably making use of the forceful but controversial trope of dividing the citizenry into good, genuine Norwegians and dishonourable, immoral or corrupt Norwegians. The radical new security policy arrangements after the war were similarly recognised by all commentators, a new orientation Norway shared with the other newcomers to NATO, Denmark and Iceland.

The contrast that Swedish history writing provides to other Nordic countries is illuminating, for it does not identify any dramatic changes in security policy arrangements during the Second World War, and in the historiography of the Swedish welfare state, linear evolution is stressed without any significant cleavages caused by the war. A linearity of this kind can also be seen in Danish history writing, whereas in Finland there is no such continuum in the historiography of the Second World War. The war changed the very parameters of Finnish welfare state reform.

The constructions of the master narratives of the Second World War thus had both differences and similarities in the Nordic countries, but we should also examine whether we can identify a breakthrough of new narratives in the last decades of the twentieth century. Where such identification is possible, were there any common elements in these new stories, and to what extent were the new narratives related to new security policy thinking? This is the second cluster of questions to be analysed. The traditional patriotic narratives created after the Second World War were produced in a security policy setting where each small nation had to pledge to a single security policy doctrine. For the NATO countries, NATO commitment was the only thinkable allegiance, whereas for Sweden and Finland, neutrality was the only alternative, although Finnish neutrality was conditioned by the obligation to be on good terms with the Soviet Union. There was little space for alternative security doctrines. Einar Maseng in Norway is a paradigmatic case of a non-conformist excluded from the public arena.[25] In Finland, the Cold War security doctrine which postulated the importance of amicable relations with the Soviet Union nevertheless did not mean that the Finnish interpretations of the Second World War corresponded to the official Soviet view. On the contrary, history writing in Finland never endorsed the Soviet theory that Finns started the Winter War in the autumn of 1939 by firing the so-called shots of Mainila. Furthermore, Finnish historians always regarded the Finnish Communist Otto Wille Kuusinen's government during the Winter War in 1939–1940, based in Terijoki in the Soviet Union, as an illegitimate puppet regime. While Finland and the Soviet Union could to a considerable degree converge on security matters, official or professional history writing differed.

A change occurred in all the Nordic countries after the dissolution of the Soviet Union. Freed from the straitjacket of one foreign policy, politicians, historians and other intellectuals as well as the general public were by the end of the century able to pass judgement on the old, canonised master narratives. In Sweden, a new generation of historians and journalists, taking for granted that there were always alternative courses of action, criticised the old interpretations for peddling the view that the Swedish government did not have any serious alternatives during the Second World

War, and argued that Sweden could have acted differently, too, to withstand Nazism. Old and new history writing in Denmark seems, on the contrary, to agree that Danes did not have much of an alternative course of action. Finnish professional historians recognised at an early stage (from the 1960s on) that the Finnish government faced a sensitive situation in how to comprehend and conceptualise collaboration with Germany and what kind of terms should be used in describing that collaboration. If there was a shift in the 1990s in the history-writing community in Finland in this regard, it boiled down to professional historians no longer talking about the Finnish war as a separate war. For their part, Norwegian history writers in this period demonstrate a fascinating plurality of interpretations, many trying to abolish the idea of a homogenous, united Norwegian population. Iceland again is a case of its own, because Icelandic history writing does not seem to demonstrate any particular shift in interpretations of the war.

And if it is possible to identify a breakthrough of new narratives on the Second World War in the last decades of the twentieth century in some of the Nordic countries, to what extent can one identify a new *moral approach* in these narratives? To what extent did the critique of the old patriotic interpretations provoke the general public and/or the history-writing community to generate polarised views? First of all, Sweden stands out as the country where the new interpretations took on a more aggressive and controversial tone than in other Nordic countries, although polarised and heated debates were also known in Norway. In Denmark, the strong consensus among professional historians was challenged not so much by the historians themselves but by politicians casting a moralistic mould of the events of the Second World War. This, the professional historians claimed, replaced source-critical interpretations of events. In Finland, the question of fighting a separate war or a war together with Germany was played up in popular debates, whereas the idea of a separate war was by now rejected by professional historians. Iceland, with an Allied military presence in the country during the war, seems not to have had any moral qualms over collaboration or active cooperation with Nazi Germany during the war years that needed to be taken into account.

Secondly, the treatment of the Holocaust constitutes a central part in the moral turn in the interpretations of the Second World War. It is obvious that the 1990s' debate in Europe on the Holocaust struck different chords in each of the Nordic countries. Iceland again appears on the sidelines of this international discourse. In Finland, the issue has recently been acknowledged by young researchers critical of a culture of silence in the Jewish question and to some extent also regarding the way history writing and the public more generally have dealt with the neighbouring Baltic states' experiences. The few historical studies on the Jews in Finland have, however, not had any particular impact on public debate. The contrast to Denmark, Norway and Sweden is remarkable: there there has been a vigorous demand to acknowledge and analyse, in a condemning tone, the role of the national historical agents of the Second World War who did not work more purposefully against the Nazis' genocidal projects. The Norwegian debate among professional historians has been especially interesting because of the interplay by respected academics claiming that the picture is not only black and white.

Finally, identifying possible changes in the interaction between professional and non-professional history writing in the different Nordic countries might shed some further light on the new narratives of the Second World War. Generally speaking, professional historians in Norway and Finland, including the most senior professors, have played a crucial role in the public debate. The situation is different in Sweden and Denmark, for while historians there occupied a strong position until the Second World War, their influence on the public debate has since waned. The critique of the patriotic narratives in Sweden was in the first instance formulated by non-historians. Somewhat differently, Finnish professional historians as well as the general public have lived with the fact that at least since the 1960s there are two interpretations or two perspectives on the Finnish engagement in the war. From the 1990s on, one can identify a cleavage in the sense that it became difficult among professional historians to defend the idea of the Finnish entanglement as a separate war. However, among the general public, including some influential members of the political elite, the idea of a separate war is as strong as ever. Such a cleavage is even more accentuated in Denmark. Professional historians are more or less agreed that there is little need in Denmark for a moral turn, while a section of the general public, and important sections of the political elite in particular, insist that a moral turn is indeed much needed. In the Norwegian case, there appears to be no obvious rupture in this question, with a frontline of professional historians on the one side and non-professionals on the other. The interpretation of Iceland's engagement in the Second World War does not seem to have caused any tensions between professional historians and the general public.

In his chapter, Bo Stråth argues that the cultural turn in history, and thereby the emergence of constructivist methodologies, resulted in the view that historians do not stand above the processes that they analyse. 'Politics took over the construction of memory.' One can certainly identify in each Nordic country a revival of interest in the national engagement in the Second World War. Popular culture (films, books and television series) has witnessed a renewed interest in the Second World War, at least in Norway and Finland, and such material makes it easy to recognise elements of the old patriotic narratives. Also, current political debates show that Danish and Swedish politicians are particularly inclined to pick up rhetorical elements from the old nationalistic story, even if they cannot find any support for such a move in the professional history writing in these countries. At the same time, the huge interest in the Second World War in Sweden demonstrates a remarkable absence of the old patriotic narrative.

New Nordic interpretations of the Second World War were linked to the democratisation process in foreign policy that had a clear connection to the end of the Cold War. But, as Stråth argues, there was no zero point in the critique of the old master narratives in the last decades of the twentieth century. Both in a broader European and a more narrow Nordic perspective, critical challenges of the grand narratives either by professional historians or media or literary figures had already begun in the 1970s. However, the critique only became *geschichtsmässig*, capable of supporting an alternative historical narrative, when it gained broader societal support in the 1990s and brought the old narratives to collapse.

Notes

1 The first part of this introduction draws on the general discussion in Johan Östling, 'Swedish Narratives of the Second World War: A European Perspective', *Contemporary European History*, 17, 2008:2.

2 See, for example, Henry Rousso, *Le syndrome de Vichy: De 1944 à nos jours* (Paris, 1987); R.J.B. Bosworth, *Explaining Auschwitz and Hiroshima: History Writing and the Second World War 1945–1990* (London, 1993); Anne Eriksen, *Det var noe annet under krigen: 2. Verdenskrig i norsk kollektivtradisjon* (Oslo, 1995); Peter Novick, *The Holocaust in American Life* (Boston, 1999); David Reynolds, *In Command of History: Churchill Fighting and Writing the Second World War* (London, 2004); and Norbert Frei, *1945 und wir: Das Dritte Reich im Bewußtsein der Deutschen* (Munich, 2005). In addition, a number of anthologies have been published, often with a transnational approach: Stig Ekman & Nils Edling (eds.), *War Experience, Self Image and National Identity: The Second World War as Myth and History* (Stockholm, 1997); Jay Winter & Emmanuel Sivan (eds.), *War and Remembrance in the Twentieth Century* (Cambridge, 1999); István Deák, Jan T. Gross & Tony Judt (eds.), *The Politics of Retribution in Europe: World War II and Its Aftermath* (Princeton, 2000); Volkhard Knigge & Norbert Frei (eds.), *Verbrechen erinnern: Die Auseinandersetzung mit Holocaust und Völkermord* (Munich, 2002); Konrad H. Jarausch & Martin Sabrow (eds.), *Verletztes Gedächtnis: Erinnerungskultur und Zeitgeschichte im Konflikt* (Frankfurt am Main, 2002); Jan-Werner Müller (ed.), *Memory and Power in Post-War Europe: Studies in the Presence of the Past* (Cambridge, 2002); Klas-Göran Karlsson & Ulf Zander (eds.), *Echoes of the Holocaust: Historical Cultures in Contemporary Europe* (Lund, 2003); Cristoph Cornelißen, Lutz Klinkhammer & Wolfgang Schwentker (eds.), *Erinnerungskulturen: Deutschland, Italien und Japan seit 1945* (Frankfurt am Main, 2003); Christoph Cornelissen (ed.), *Diktatur – Krieg – Vertreibung: Erinnerungskulturen in Tschechien, der Slowakei und Deutschland seit 1945* (Essen, 2005); Klas-Göran Karlsson & Ulf Zander (eds.), *The Holocaust on Post-War Battlefields: Genocide as Historical Culture* (Lund, 2006); Robert Bohn, Christoph Cornelissen & Karl Christian Lammers (eds.), *Vergangenheitspolitik und Erinnerungskulturen im Schatten des Zweiten Weltkriegs: Deutschland und Skandinavien seit 1945* (Essen, 2008); Elena Lamberti & Vita Fortunati (eds.), *Memories and Representations of War: The Case of World War I and World War II* (Amsterdam, 2009); Małgorzata Pakier & Bo Stråth (eds.), *A European Memory?: Contested Histories and Politics of Remembrance* (New York, 2010). In terms of comparative and overall views of national narratives of the Second World War, however, one work is indispensable: Monika Flacke (ed.), *Mythen der Nationen: 1945 – Arena der Erinnerungen*, 2 vols. (Berlin, 2004).

3 Konrad H. Jarausch & Michael Geyer, *Shattered Past: Reconstructing German Histories* (Princeton, 2003), viii.

4 Pieter Lagrou, *The Legacy of Nazi Occupation: Patriotic Memory and National Recovery in Western Europe, 1945–1965* (Cambridge, 2000). See also Pieter Lagrou, 'Victims of Genocide and National Memory: Belgium, France and the Netherlands 1945–1965', *Past and Present*, 154, 1997:1.

5 Claus Bryld & Anette Warring, *Besættelsestiden som kollektiv erindring* (Roskilde, 1999).
6 Mark Mazower, *Dark Continent: Europe's Twentieth Century* (London, 1998), 215–216.
7 Etienne François, 'Meistererzählungen und Dammbrüche: Die Erinnerung an den Zweiten Weltkrieg zwischen Nationalisierung und Universalisierung', in: Monika Flacke (ed.), *Mythen der Nationen: 1945 – Arena der Erinnerungen*, 2 vols. (Berlin, 2004), 14–18.
8 François 2004, 16–20.
9 François 2004, 17. See also Martin Conway & Peter Romijn, 'Introduction', *Contemporary European History*, 13, 2004:4, 377–388.
10 Tony Judt, *Postwar: A History of Europe since 1945* (London, 2005), 61–62 and 803–831.
11 Ulrich Beck, 'The Cosmopolitan Society and Its Enemies', *Theory, Culture and Society*, 2002:1–2.
12 François 2004, 17–18.
13 Rousso 1987.
14 See, for example, Frei 2005.
15 François 2004, 19–25. The Holocaust in contemporary European history culture is analysed in Klas-Göran Karlsson, 'The Holocaust as a Problem of Historical Culture', in: Klas-Göran Karlsson & Ulf Zander (eds.), *Echoes of the Holocaust: Historical Cultures in Contemporary Europe* (Lund, 2003).
16 François 2004, 21–22.
17 Uffe Østergård, 'Denmark and the New International Politics of Morality and Remembrance', in: Per Carlsen & Hans Mouritzen (eds.), *Danish Foreign Policy Yearbook 2005* (Copenhagen, 2005), 6.
18 This organisation promotes education, remembrance and research about the Holocaust and genocide studies both nationally and internationally; Østergård 2005, 5.
19 Doris Bachmann-Medick, *Cultural Turns: Neuorientierungen in den Kulturwissenschaften* (Reinbek, 2006).
20 George Cotkin, 'History's Moral Turn', *Journal of the History of Ideas*, 69, 2008:2, 295–304.
21 Norman Davies, *Europe at War 1939–1945: No Simple Victory* (London, 2006), 471–472, 478–479.
22 Dag Anckar, 'Demokrati och utrikespolitik', *Politiikka*, 26, 1984:1, 64–71; Herbert Tingsten, *Svensk utrikesdebatt mellan världskrigen* (Stockholm, 1964), 321.
23 Kjell Goldmann, 'Swedish Policy Making on International Questions: Bureaucratization and Politization', in: Kjell Goldmann, Sten Berglund & Gunnar Sjöstedt, *Democracy and Foreign Policy: The Case of Sweden* (Aldershot, 1986), 164, 173. See also Tingsten 1964, 318.
24 Tero Erkkilä, 'Reinventing Nordic Openness: Transparency and State Information in Finland', *Acta Politica*, 40, 2010, 210.
25 Lars Mjøset, 'Introduksjon: Einar Masengs politiske biografi', in: Einar Maseng,

Utsikt over de nordeuropeiske staters utenrikspolitikk i de siste århundrer, vol. I (Oslo, 2005); Lars Mjøset, 'Etterord: Einar Masengs analyse av Norden i det europeiske statssystemet', in: Einar Maseng, *Utsikt over de nord-europeiske staters utenrikspolitikk i de siste århundrer*, vol. III (Oslo, 2005).

CHAPTER 2

Swords, Shields or Collaborators?

Danish Historians and the Debate over the German Occupation of Denmark

Uffe Østergård

This chapter analyses the changing interpretations of the German occupation of Denmark during the Second World War in a comparative frame. Surprisingly, there is not much of a tradition of comparing the historical experiences of the Nordic countries either during the Second World War or in other contexts. This is probably because developments in these countries have been understood as similar, not requiring any explicit comparisons. The main exception seems to be comparative studies of the welfare state. Yet, the endeavour to compare the Nordic countries is most worthwhile, as shown in the first in-depth analysis of the experiences of Denmark and Norway during the Second World War.[1] The two countries have been treated as parallel cases and their different experiences have only been compared in the thorough introduction by Hans Fredrik Dahl and Hans Kirchhoff.[2] We should clearly do much more in the area of explicit comparison, something that has been attempted in another recent anthology of interdisciplinary studies in the history and memory in the Nordic countries.[3]

The main result of my reading of the Danish debates over the Second World War is that of a fundamental contrast between the results of the professional historians and of the reading public, among them many politicians. The confrontation was brought out in the open in what amounts to a Danish version of the German *Historikerstreit* of 1986–1988 under Anders Fogh Rasmussen's centre-right government in the early 2000s. But the confrontation reflects a much older tradition of populism – *folkelighed* in Danish – and mistrust of all elites.

What followed immediately after the war was an interpretative consensus on wartime Denmark. In this understanding, the resistance movement was interpreted as a sword directed against the German occupation, while the policies of the cooperating – or collaborating – politicians were seen as providing a shield of protection to the majority of the population, including the Danish Jews who were rescued in 1943. Professional historians have challenged this grand narrative in various ways since the 1950s, and while their books have sold relatively well, they have apparently not dented popular belief to any great extent.

Only the populist turn and the interventions of the Prime Minister in 2003 and 2005 have politicised the previous consensus and somewhat belatedly opened the door for a 'moral turn' in occupation studies. Already in the 1990s investigations of the importance of Danish industry and agriculture for the German war effort, treatment of women fraternising with the Germans, asylum-seeking refugees and the like, had begun to change the overall picture of Denmark during the war. The 'moral turn' has not yet been fully accepted by the public, except from one item: the fact that some of the fishermen who helped Jews escaping to Sweden benefitted economically from their apparent altruism. How the debate over the memory of the occupation will develop in future depends mainly on the success of the activist Danish foreign policy characterised by participation in military interventions in various parts of the world.

The Beginnings of the Master Narrative

The discussion of how Danish society adapted to the German occupation in 1940–1945 began almost immediately after the German invasion of Denmark on 9 April 1940 and has continued ever since, albeit with varying intensity. Was it at all possible to defend

Denmark by military means? And if the armed forces seriously had fought back, would they have fought in the right places, or would they have concentrated on traditional land-military defence at Vejle Ådal in Jutland instead of protecting the main target of the German forces, Ålborg airfield in northern Jutland, which the German military needed for the campaign against Norway? Was the Danish capitulation an expression of cowardice, perhaps an expression of a defeatist national character? Or was the acceptance of German occupation on top of Denmark's virtual demilitarisation in the inter-war period part of an alternative and coherent strategy of a societal defence of democratic and human values? Was the Danish accommodation to German interests in the 1930s and the subsequent 'policy of cooperation' – or 'policy of collaboration' – with the German occupying regime during the war morally defensible?

The concept *samarbejdspolitik* (policy of cooperation) was the standard designation of Danish wartime policy under Nazi occupation by its critics in the illegal press. When used by politicians, the term implied that the Danish politicians collaborated across party lines in the national interests. In order to describe their lack of independence, they used the term *tilpasningspolitik* (policy of adaptation) or *indrømmelsespolitik* (policy of accommodation), which I have chosen as an apt English compromise between the different terms. The Danish term *kollaboration* (collaboration) is generally restricted to the active furthering of the enemy cause during wartime. Whether the official Danish policy should really be interpreted as a policy of collaboration, which was the line taken, for example, by the historian Hans Kirchhoff in 1979, is still debated.[4] Kirchhoff himself modified his original vehement denunciation of the official policy in 2001 when discussing the correct terminology regarding the Danish policy.[5] In a recent publication in English on the history of twentieth-century Denmark, another influential historian, Bo Lidegaard, has chosen the term 'cooperation'.[6]

The discussion concerning the Second World War began during the occupation and continued with the trials against collaborators from the summer of 1945 until 1948. The debate then gradually ebbed away, relegated to a parliamentary commission established on 15 June 1945. The commission concluded its work in 1953 with a comprehensive report in fourteen volumes, consisting of 14,000 pages with stacks of documents and accounts.[7] After this the discussion shifted to professional historians, who organised themselves as the so-called Publication Society for Danish Contemporary History (*Udgiverselskabet for Danmarks Nyere Historie*, DNH) in 1960.

The dominant figure in the professional research on the occupation period was Jørgen Hæstrup (1909–1998). Without really feeling at home in the academic environment at the history department at the University of Copenhagen, Hæstrup took a degree in history in 1934 and became a high school teacher at Skt. Knuds Gymnasium in Odense. During the occupation, he was active in the resistance. He went underground in September 1944 and spent the rest of the occupation in Copenhagen. In 1947, Hæstrup began to collect material about the Danish resistance movement, using the data for his doctoral thesis *Kontakt med England 1940–1943* ('Contact with England, 1940–1943'), which he defended at Aarhus University in 1954. He depicted the resistance movement as having a significant role during the occupation, which pleased the many resistance fighters who attended his dissertation defence. It was less important that the official opponents at the defence, professors C.O. Bøggild-Andersen from Aarhus and Sven Henningsen of Copenhagen University, expressed strong criticism of his use of the sources and other aspects of methodology.

In a follow-up study from 1959, entitled *Hemmelig alliance* ('Secret alliance'), Hæstrup produced the classic interpretation of the Danish resistance movement, de-emphasising contradictions between the movement's Conservative, Social Democratic and Communist members. Instead, he concentrated on the so-called 'distorted distribution of British weapons' between active resistance fighters and what he considered the inactive, anti-Communist officer group (known as 'Ogroups') who obtained the most weapons. This led Martin Nielsen, editor of the Danish Communist Party newspaper *Land og Folk,* to accuse the army chief of staff Lieutenant General Viggo Hjalf of treason, at which Hjalf sued Nielsen for libel. Nielsen lost, served three months in prison, and paid a large sum in compensation. However, a debate in the Danish parliament, *Folketinget*, led to Hjalf's early retirement. The two volumes, *Kontakt med England*

1940–1943 and *Hemmelig alliance* were eventually published in English in 1976–1977 as a single volume entitled *Secret Alliance.*

The predominant narrative about Danish politics during the occupation, 'the war of the entire people' against Germany and Nazism during the Second World War, was established very rapidly even before the war ended. The activities of the politicians and high-ranking civil servants (*departementscheferne*) were interpreted as a 'shield' that protected the population against the worst, while the resistance movement was viewed as a 'sword' directed against the occupying power. This effort saved the Danish position at the last minute, placing Denmark on the side of the victorious Allies as co-founder of the United Nations in the summer of 1945. How this move was possible for a country which in real terms had been allied with Nazi Germany until the summer of 1943 at least, almost beats imagination. Much of the success of the manoeuvre depended on the fact that the majority of the Jews in Denmark, by good luck, were saved from Nazi persecution in October 1943. The legal fig leaf for the policy of accommodation was provided by the creation of the logically contradictory label 'peace occupation' for the situation after the German invasion on 9 April 1940. Regardless of the fact that until August 1943 most of official Denmark had condemned and persecuted the resistance fighters – and some even longer – the last months of the war and the first six months of peace witnessed the formation of a successful alliance between the resistance movement and the politicians, which soon brought Denmark back to normal and reduced the war experience to an exotic parenthesis.[8]

After Hæstrup had pursued his research for many years largely as a hobby, his situation changed when the DNH[9] launched a thorough investigation of the history of the occupation period, accompanied by a generous grant from the state and privileged access to the national archives. In 1961, Jørgen Hæstrup became the academic co-director of the society together with national archivist Johan Hvidtfeldt. In 1965, DNH was able to publish *Besættelsens Hvem-Hvad-Hvor* ('The who, what and where of the Occupation'), and in 1966, Hæstrup's own *Til landets bedste ... Hovedtræk af departementchefsstyrets virke 1943–1945* ('For the good of the country... Main characteristics of the work of the permanent secretaries' administration 1943–1945').

To the surprise of many members of the resistance, Hæstrup defended the administration of the permanent secretaries after the cessation of cooperation in August 1943, when the cabinet ministers withdrew and the Parliament ceased to function. In Hæstrup's view, these officials operated as a virtual appendage to the resistance movement, providing a 'shield' for the 'sword' of the resistance. Hæstrup thus provided a scholarly version of the understanding of the Danish policy under occupation that had already been formulated in the summer of 1945, when the politicians resumed power in cooperation with selected representatives from the resistance. This 'consensus line' saw the occupation as marked by a broad consensus: almost the entire Danish population resisted the German occupation power, even if there was disagreement on the means of the struggle.

This 'master narrative', as the interpretation has been baptised by the historians Claus Bryld and Anette Warring, is not exclusively Danish, although it has often been portrayed as such.[10] It corresponds surprisingly well to the myths of the importance of the resistance in most occupied countries in Western Europe as depicted by the British historian Tony Judt in his masterly 2005 synthesis of Europe's post-war history, *Postwar*. Judt draws attention to the reverse relationship between the real importance of the resistance and the myth that came to surround it. In his own words:

> The only source of collective national pride were the armed partisan resistance movements that had fought the invader – which is why it was in western Europe, where the real resistance had actually been least in evidence, that the myth of Resistance mattered most. In Greece, Yugoslavia, Poland or Ukraine, where large numbers of real partisans had engaged the occupation forces and each other in open battle, things were, as usual more complicated. [...] 'Resistance', in short, was a protean and unclear category, in some places an invented one. But 'collaboration' was another matter. Collaborators could be universally identified and execrated.[11]

This observation led Judt to his only comments about Denmark during the Second World War: 'In Denmark the crime of collaboration was virtually unknown. Yet 374 out of every 100,000 Danes were sentenced to prison in post-war trials. In France, where wartime collaboration was widespread, it was for just that reason punished rather lightly.'[12] Such large-scale comparisons have only recently been introduced into the study of Danish occupation history.

The Grand Narrative Under Attack – The Second Generation of Historians

The consensus line has since been challenged in various ways by some of the representatives of the second generation of historians who had been DNH-trained by Hæstrup. In 1995, Henning Poulsen, professor at Aarhus University, somewhat cynically summed up the Danish war experience as follows:

> We collaborated politically with the occupation power and achieved conditions that, in comparison with other occupied countries, were good and relatively free. We then got a resistance movement at half price, and, finally, we became an allied power without entering the war.[13]

Other prominent members of this second generation of historians, all born in the early 1930s, were Henrik Nissen of Copenhagen University and Aage Trommer of Odense University (now part of the University of Southern Denmark). The most productive of them, though, is Hans Kirchhoff, who denounced the Danish wartime policy as 'collaboration' in his 1979 dissertation focusing on the anti-German near-rebellions all over the country in August 1943 except in the capital, Copenhagen. In 2001, Kirchhoff collected his life's research in *Samarbejde og modstand under besættelsen: En politisk historie* ('Cooperation and resistance during the occupation: A political history'). A superb synthesis of a long career dedicated to the 1940–1945 occupation period, the book demonstrated that interesting history is not written (only) by journalists.

In the extensive bibliography entitled *Samarbejde og modstand: Danmark under den tyske besættelse 1940–45: En bibliografi* ('Cooperation and resistance: Denmark during the German occupation 1940–45: A bibliography') from the Royal Library in 2002, Kirchhoff is the most prolific with 117 entries, not including newspaper articles. He and his generation cannot be accused of having ignored the wider public and of reserving their findings for an exclusive scholarly community of fellow historians. On the contrary, they went on television as early as the late 1960s, producing a whole series of programmes on the Second World War. Their books were always reviewed at length in the newspapers and inevitably attracted critical interest from the general public and surviving members of the resistance movement in particular. Yet, their criticism of the dominating consensus narrative of a united Danish front of resistance against the Germans never really caught on, even though their books sold in relatively large numbers.

Communication to the broader public outside the narrow circle of professional historians has always been a significant element in Kirchhoff's work. There is virtually no media in which he has made known his own results and those of his many students. The highpoint thus far is the collection of essays mentioned above, *Samarbejde og modstand under besættelsen*, which provides an extremely well-crafted synthesis for the broader public and covers the period that has preoccupied Kirchhoff through a long professional life. The work has taken its place in the current debate and represents a profound break with what he termed the use – and especially abuse – of contemporary history in the 1990s and the first decade of the twenty-first century. In the preface, Kirchhoff writes:

> Good colleagues tell me that the grand theme of the occupation concerning cooperation or resistance is out, that the research stands at a crossroads and is drying up, and that it can survive only by focusing on other questions such as human rights and Europeanisation, which are in today. I do not agree, and I also think that the intense media debate on the policy of cooperation in these years repudiates this judgement. As I see it, it is more important than ever, now that the generation of the occupation years is dying out, that the historians intervene in a discussion which so often obtains the character of an ahistorical attack on the line of cooperation and a superficial embrace of the resistance point of view, which has now become gratuitous following the

> fall of the [Berlin] Wall. This book can be seen as a contribution to such a necessary historicization.[14]

In a subsequent anthology of fourteen portraits of people who chose opposite policies, Kirchhoff provides an exquisite summary of the predominant point of view among the majority of professional historians, regardless of generation:

> A pervasive theme in the book is the choice between cooperation and resistance, that which in the confused debate of our day seems to be so easy and uncomplicated. With 70 years of distance, we would all certainly say that there ought to have been resistance from the first day of the occupation! To this one can say that all the occupied countries cooperated or *collaborated* with the enemy during the Second World War, regardless of whether they were occupied peacefully such as Denmark, or were occupied following war and conquest. Negotiations had to take place with foreign troops in the country, and everyday life had to go on [...] Collaboration in the hour of defeat became France's response to German occupation, a response supported by the vast majority. But with the Allies' victory and the growth of the resistance movement, collaboration became synonymous with treason, and in the final settling of the accounts after the war, collaborators were shot and executed en masse. A similar development took place in occupied and liberated Europe, where, in the summer of liberation of 1945, it could lead to loss of life or in any case to losing a career to have been on the wrong side. Therefore, only very few defended collaboration in its own right as the legitimate response of the weak to the attack by the superpower Germany, and as a choice between a greater or a lesser evil. This resulted in a European myth of cooperation as a form of hidden resistance, a myth that has clouded the discussion right up to the present day.
>
> In a sociological perspective, all the citizens in the occupied countries participated in the collaboration by producing and working and driving for the Germans. They may have been clenching their fists in their pockets, but they followed the Germans' directives and were thus helping to make the occupation easier for them. Only

a small minority chose to resist. The vast majority were primarily occupied with personal matters, with family, work and providing food. As we know, the instinct for self-preservation is not the most noble of goals, but it is the most basic!

To all appearances, there was never any choice in Denmark between cooperation and resistance for the majority of the population. For the most part, people heeded the message of the King and the Government for peace and order and without major problems supported the war programme of the Freedom Council [*Frihedsrådet*]. Neither did there exist any choice for the official Denmark, that is, the politicians, civil servants, business, organisations and the press, who supported the line of cooperation to the bitter end as the only correct policy which could protect against the misfortunes of war and German repression. Those who turned to active resistance were exceptions confirming the rule that, all things considered, the path to illegal struggle was longer for a politician, police chief or trade union boss than for a schoolteacher, machinist or shop assistant. One need only be reminded that most of the Freedom Council were unbound and free intellectuals. What distinguished them was their social role, that which Max Weber has called the 'ethic of *responsibility*' as opposed to the 'ethic of *conviction*'. The dilemma is of a deep moral and existential nature, and it existed throughout occupied Europe, where resistance could provoke retribution leading to death and destruction of innocent people.[15]

The Politics of History – A Danish 'Historikerstreit'

Alternative narratives of the war existed, but they remained marginal until the late 1990s, even though some of the Communist narratives gained great popularity in the teaching of Danish history and literature in secondary schools (primarily Hans Scherfig's novel *Frydenholm* from 1962). Criticism of the 'policy of accommodation' became more vocal only with the fall of Communism and in the face of an emerging activist Danish foreign policy from the early 1990s onward, which entailed Danish participation in the NATO bombing of Serbia in the Kosovo crisis in 1999 and the interventions in Afghanistan in 2002 onwards and in Iraq in

2003–2007. The liberal-conservative Prime Minister Anders Fogh Rasmussen has successfully formulated a new narrative about Danish neutrality policy in the twentieth century which seems to have carried the day.

Apart from specific polemics, which tended to flare up in conjunction with the publication of historical research, the discussion over the occupation years, somewhat paradoxically, only resurfaced after the end of the Cold War in the 1990s. In 1995, the fiftieth anniversary of the end of the Second World War triggered a public debate about the appropriateness of commemorating the end of the war on 5 May 1945 with a laser beam from bunker to bunker along the west coast of Jutland, which had been fortified to ward off an invasion that never came.[16] However, a fundamental critique of the wartime policy of accommodation was only formulated by responsible decision-makers after the election of a centre-right coalition government in 2001 (with the support of the nationalist-populist Danish People's Party).

This change of government marked a radical departure from the centre-left coalition of Social Democrats and Social Liberals which had ruled for a decade and had generally dominated Danish politics since 1929. In this new constellation, Prime Minister Anders Fogh Rasmussen of the Liberal party *Venstre* officially condemned what he called the 'cowardly policy of cooperation'. His initiative may seem slightly out of place as his party has traditionally represented the interests of the farmers who had profited most from the occupation, when Denmark supplied the German war effort with agricultural products. Anders Fogh Rasmussen held a symbolically laden speech in 2003 at the Naval Academy to mark the sixtieth anniversary of the end of the official policy of accommodation in August 1943. He expressed his condemnation of Denmark's acquiescence in 1940 and of the subsequent policy of toleration of the German Occupation which until then had been defended by most politicians. It must be taken into account that the main political reason for Rasmussen's statements was his wish to mobilise support for the interventionist Danish foreign policy after 2001, which culminated in Danish participation in the American-led invasions of Afghanistan in 2002 and Iraq in 2003. The intervention in Iraq, in contrast to the foreign policy activism of the 1990s, most notably Denmark's participation in NATO's 1999 bombing of Serbia in support of Kosovo's independence, was based on a narrow majority in parliament and is still very controversial. In contrast to most other participating countries, however, it is still not much debated.

Anders Fogh Rasmussen's speech in 2003, which is discussed below and is available in Danish on the 'About 1945' homepage of the Ministry of Education (published in 2005), should thus be primarily read as a contribution to a domestic political debate over Danish foreign policy. But his views extended far beyond the present political situation, which has led to a confrontation with the professional historians, who almost unanimously rejected the Prime Minister's contribution to the debate as the ahistorical wisdom of hindsight. They saw it as a condemnation of his predecessors' choices without any attempt to appreciate the difficult situation in which they found themselves and the background to the choices they made in a situation where they had no support from the Allies. The discussion must be seen as an extension of the Prime Minister's contest with the intellectual elite in general in his campaign against what were called 'arbiters of taste' (*smagsdommere*), a campaign he declared in his New Year's address on 1 January 2002, shortly after taking office. However, Fogh Rasmussen's speech is also connected with the fact that aside from a brief Marxist flirtation in the 1970s, most of the Danish historians, ever since the professionalisation of the discipline at the universities in the 1880s, have been very closely linked to a single political party, the Social Liberals of *Radikale Venstre*.[17] The dominant figure, and also a prominent politician, was Peter Munch, or Dr P. Munch, as he preferred to be called. As minister of defence during the First World War and as foreign minister from 1929 to 1940, Munch had been responsible for the foreign and security policy denounced by critics as the 'German course'.[18] With few exceptions, post-war historians of all political persuasions have shown an understanding for the policy conducted during the war, even though some, among them Hans Kirchhoff, chose to call the policy of cooperation by its correct European name of collaboration.[19]

Fogh Rasmussen's reinterpretation is linked to the nationalist position expressed by the theologians in the Danish religious movement *Tidehverv* (literally 'New Era'), a current that forms the ideological basis of the Danish People's Party's political success.[20] However, the fact that the position has also gained ground within the Liberal Party, which during the occupation represented those agricultural interests that profited so much from cooperation with Nazi Germany,[21] is surprising, to say the least. That such a change is possible testifies to a lack of historical consciousness, or at least a lack of continuity, in Danish political culture. At the same time, however, it shows that the professional historians do not exercise a monopoly on interpretation of the past. One can discuss whether they have ever had such a monopoly. It is enough to think of the outcry that has occurred each time the second generation of historians of the occupation demonstrated how few persons were actually involved in the resistance, or how little effect their actions had on the course of the war. Today, however, it has become clear that the historians no longer determine how the Second World War is remembered and which lessons can be learned from this important episode in the national narrative.

The majority of Danish historians, as mentioned, have rejected the activist reinterpretation of the message of the Second World War. One can almost speak of a Danish *Historikerstreit* on a par with the German debate in 1986–1988 over war guilt and suffering. The debate between politicians and professional historians broke out in 2003 with a commentary in the Social Liberal newspaper *Politiken* by the historian Niels Wium Olesen from Aarhus University. Olesen belongs to what we can call the third generation of occupation historians. He previously headed the Collection for Occupation-era History in Esbjerg and has co-authored the most authoritative and balanced investigation of all sides of the occupation period together with Claus Bundgård Christensen, Joachim Lund and Jakob Sørensen (all three born in the late 1960s or early 1970s). Their book, *Danmark besat: Krig og hverdag 1940–45* ('Denmark occupied: War and everyday life 1940–1945') , first appeared in 2005. Their basic view of the Danish policy of accommodation resembles Kirchhoff's nuanced judgement.[22]

The historians' detailed and empathetic judgement of the Danish occupation, compared with the situation in other occupied countries in Europe, stands in fundamental contrast to Fogh Rasmussen's condemnation of the Danish policy as collaborationist. In his 2003 Naval Academy speech, Fogh Rasmussen declared:

> 29 August 1943 is a date we should remember – and be proud of. On that day, Denmark's honour was saved. The Danish government finally stopped cooperating with the German occupying powers and resigned. After three years of cooperation with the Germans, clearly defined lines were finally drawn. Nor was it a day too soon [...] The government, the *Folketing* and the established Denmark did not benefit from the cessation of cooperation with the Germans. On the contrary, the official Denmark, from the start of the occupation of Denmark on 9 April 1940, had obediently complied with the Germans, cooperated on all levels, and encouraged the population to do the same. In taking up the post of Foreign Minister in 1940, Erik Scavenius declared that 'the great German victories' had 'struck the world with amazement and admiration'. He concluded that Denmark should now find its place in a necessary and mutually active cooperation with the Germans. It was not enough that Denmark's political leadership decided to follow a passive policy of cooperation in relation to the Germans. The government at the time consciously and openly chose an active policy toward the occupying power in the hope that some of the sovereignty would be respected. Recent historical research reveals that it was in fact a case of a very active cooperation policy. Many were convinced of a German victory. Politicians, officials and organisations began to prepare for Denmark's place in a new, Nazi-dominated Europe. Centrally placed officials worked on plans to transform the Danish economy following the Nazi planned-economy pattern.
>
> The main argument for the policy of cooperation was that all Danish resistance against the German superpower was useless. By cooperating with the occupying power, Denmark and the Danish population were sheltered from most of the horrors of war. And it succeeded. The Danes escaped the worst destruction. Agriculture and industry profited from the war. Viewed on the basis of such a

cold calculation, some people might perhaps call the cooperation policy necessary, clever and appropriate. But this is a very dangerous way of thinking. If everyone had thought like the Danish cooperation politicians, Hitler would in all probability have won the war, and Europe would have become Nazi. But fortunately, the British and later the Americans and Russians did not think like the Danish elite. They fought a life-and-death struggle against the Nazis and thereby secured our freedom. In the final analysis, it was the population's growing dissatisfaction with the cooperation policy and the efforts of the courageous members of the resistance that forced the government to renounce cooperation with the Germans. We should be happy about this, and proud of it. We owe a great debt of thanks to the resistance fighters who, through sabotage against the Germans and cooperation with the Allies, defied the cooperating politicians and ultimately ensured Denmark its place on the right side of the struggle against the Nazis.

Naturally, one should be cautious in making a judgement about the past on the basis of the present. Today we know that the Nazis lost the war after the US and the Soviet Union became involved in 1941, and therefore the active Danish policy of cooperation appears as mistaken and contemptible. If it had been continued until the end of the war, Denmark would have appeared as a German client state and ally. In the light of history, it would have been a catastrophe. But did things appear differently at the start of the war? If the Germans had indeed won, would Denmark not have profited in adapting itself to the German dominance in time? Many people thought so. However, it appears naive to think that Hitler would have given special consideration to Denmark in the event of a German victory. There were also highly placed officials who from the very beginning of the war had distanced themselves from these naive ideas. Denmark's independent emissary in Washington Henrik Kaufmann and the counsellor to the Danish legation in Berlin Vincens Steensen-Leth realised from the outset that the policy of cooperation was naive and mistaken. They warned that Denmark would never obtain concessions from the Nazis, neither on this point or that, because it was the very idea of the democratic state of law that the Nazis wanted to kill off. The Nazis accepted only

> one form of system, the national socialist form. There was no room for special treatment in what Hitler called the 'clattering of small states'. Even judging by the assumptions of the time, the Danish policy appears naive, and it is very contemptible that the political elite in Denmark conducted not only a policy of neutrality, but acted with such a degree of active adaptation to German interests.
>
> In the struggle between democracy and dictatorship, one cannot be neutral. One must take a stand for democracy and against dictatorship. It is on this point that the active policy of active adaptation constituted a political and moral failure. All too often in history, we Danes have sailed under a flag of convenience and allowed others to fight for our freedom and peace. The lesson from 29 August 1943 is that if our values of freedom, democracy and human rights are to be meant seriously, then we ourselves must also make an active contribution to defending them. Also against difficult odds, even when unpopular and dangerous decisions have to be made. Thank you.[23]

As can be seen, the Prime Minister's condemnation of the policy of cooperation is not without reference to recent historical research. This is hardly surprising considering the fact that one of his closest staff members at the time was the historian Bo Lidegaard, who has written a very successful book on Denmark in the 1930s and 1940s, which interestingly contradicts the interpretation of his political boss. Fogh Rasmussen simply chose to disagree and to ignore the historicising relativism of most historians in favour of a contemporary political judgement intended to justify Danish participation in the wars in Afghanistan and Iraq.

Yet, Anders Fogh Rasmussen's condemnation of the policy of accommodation does not represent a complete breach with the grand narrative. On the contrary, after the liberation, almost all politicians, with the exception of the honourably steadfast Social Democrats Hartvig Frisch and Hal Koch, sought to distance themselves from their positions during the occupation and embraced the resistance movement. The sword and shield metaphor had, as previously shown, become central in the Danish collective remembrance of the war. It fused the two policies as supplementing variants of resistance, where disagreement was only about the means. What was new was the unequivocal moral condemnation of the cooperation arrangement, a moralism about the past in which Fogh Rasmussen was far from unique (see, for instance, Hans Kirchhoff's speech on accepting the H.O. Lange prize for the popularising of research in 2001 and his book published in the same year).

In fact, one can conclude that while the professional historians have won out on the book front, they appear to have lost the battle for public opinion. Books abound about the Second World War, defending the policy of accommodation as the only political option for a small country that had been delivered up to the mercy of the German great power, books which explore the dilemmas from all possible angles. Some of them, such as Bo Lidegaard's work from 2005, sell in very large numbers. At the same time, however, the majority of politicians and possibly the majority of the voters support the activist attitude, which condemns 'the policy of accommodation' as morally abominable and as an expression of cowardice from which we have fortunately recovered following the end of the Cold War and, most notably, with the help of the centre-right coalition government in 2001. Historians' nuances and understanding of the impossible choices in the past apparently play a minuscule role in the debate over Danish public opinion at the beginning of the third millennium. It is as if the Danes of today are fighting the war our predecessors neglected to fight between 1940 and 1945 – apart from the fact that Denmark made a decisive contribution by supplying Germany with agricultural products and with volunteers for the Waffen SS.[24]

Virtually all professional historians in Denmark seem united in their understanding of the policies during the Second World War, an understanding which differs fundamentally from the basic narrative held by the rest of the population, no matter whether it is the older consensus narrative or the former Prime Minister's moral(istic) condemnation of the policy of cooperation. There is only one feature of the war experience which seems to be remembered in the same way – the rescue of the Jews.

Holocaust in Denmark?

The rescue of the Danish Jews in October 1943 is a major and unrivalled event in Danish history, laying the foundation for Denmark's humanitarian reputation. The rescue is internationally recognised to a remarkable degree, both at the Yad Vashem Institute in Jerusalem and the Holocaust Memorial Museum in Washington. Both exhibitions contain an original fishing boat which took Danish Jews across the Øresund Strait to Sweden, along with inscriptions thanking the people of Denmark for their heroic deeds. This collective expression of thanks has a particularly strong effect, since otherwise only individuals recorded by name are given prominence in Yad Vashem's memorial park. In her famous book on the trial of Eichmann in Jerusalem, published in 1963, Hannah Arendt singled out Denmark as a small, 'stubborn' country where it proved impossible for the Nazis to make people accept their perverted ideas about their Jewish fellow citizens.

The spontaneous popular efforts by Danes to save the Danish Jews can be regarded as an expression of those virtues and values which Danes want to associate with everything Danish. Seen in light of what Denmark otherwise contributed to the Second World War, as a passive occupied country whose government accommodated the German occupation and supplied Germany with food and other important products, it may be said that this popular contribution redressed the balance, compensating for the cowardice and outright collaboration of official Denmark during the occupation. For a long period, the Allies had good reason to question whether Denmark should be classified as an ally of Germany or as an opponent. By the skin of its teeth, Denmark was included in the group of allied victors when the United Nations was founded in 1945. As we have seen, questions about Denmark's position during the war have been raised in recent public debates. New generations of historians and journalists have investigated the extent and the enthusiasm with which Danish business circles complied with the German side, an effort which even included Danish participation in the German exploitation of the conquered territories in Eastern Europe, including the use of forced labour in some Danish-run factories in Estonia and elsewhere.[25] That the participation of Danish businesses in the war effort was complemented by the participation of Danish volunteers in Waffen SS units has been convincingly demonstrated by recent research.[26]

The rescue of the Danish Jews does not wipe the stain from the Danish national conscience. However, it serves as recompense for the lack of a moral stand on the part of a small state in the most crucial test of strength in the twentieth century. The saving of the Jews shows what people are capable of when they share the same values and the same political culture. The rescue also demonstrates the importance of individuals when they commit themselves. 'Courage to care', as it is known in international Holocaust education. Yet, while some Danish self-praise is justified, it is important to remember the conditions that enabled Danes to rescue the Jews, especially when compared with the situation in other small or medium-sized countries such as the Netherlands and Norway.

First, there were differences between the Danish and Dutch situations. Danes could more easily rescue Danish Jews because the shores of Sweden were so close by (an hour or less by small craft) and because Sweden itself was neutral. The presence of a close, neutral neighbour and the geography of Zealand are the main reasons why things turned out so differently for Jews in Denmark than for the Jews in the Netherlands. The extermination of the Dutch Jews has left an open wound in the collective Dutch memory that is not treatable with excuses. However, Danes should remember that it was infinitely more difficult to help Jews in hiding for many years than helping them cross from Denmark to Sweden. Moreover, the Dutch suffered under a much harsher Nazi regime, led by the fanatical Austrian Arthur Seyss-Inquart. This difference in war experience has been an important factor in explaining the great difference in attitude between Denmark and the Netherlands after the Second World War. Nevertheless, the two countries share many similar views and values, and their structural position and interests as small states in Europe are certainly comparable.

A second factor behind the Danish success in rescuing its Jewish citizens compared to the Dutch relates to the conflicting attitudes within the German occupying power in the two countries. The German *Wehrmacht* had no interest in provoking resistance in Denmark, as this could have changed a situation that in fact continued unaltered until the end of the occupation. Such stability allowed the Germans to use Denmark as a base where exhausted soldiers could rest and recuperate. German soldiers called Denmark the 'cream front' (*Sahnefront* or *flødeskumsfronten*), where they were sent to recover from battles elsewhere. The Danish population did not see the situation in this light, but for German soldiers, Denmark was a comfortable billet where they could regain their strength after the horrors of the Eastern Front. Moreover, not all German officers shared the Nazi regime's anti-Semitic ideology. They saw no reason to carry out the strict orders and hunt down those whom both they and the Danish population regarded as Danish citizens, that is, citizens of a nation that was not at war with Germany. This attitude was not known to the organisers of the escape routes nor to those who fled. And it certainly does not detract in any way from the heroism shown by those who rescued the Danish Jews. However, the success of the Danish rescue lies in the fact that the Germans were not that interested in capturing the fleeing Jews.

Something else we can learn from the attitude of the Danish population during the Second World War, and which has a more general relevance than the actual rescue of the Jews, is the Danish population's relative immunity to totalitarian ideologies. Even during the Nazi occupation, and with the privileges which would accrue to a Danish Nazi, the Danish Nazi Party only managed to attract less than 2 per cent of the vote in the free elections of March 1943. Even though Communists were not allowed to stand for election, the turnout was 89.5 per cent, the highest ever recorded. The five parties of the old coalition government won 94.5 per cent of the vote. The Communists would probably not have received many votes at the time, even if they had been allowed to stand. The many votes received by the Communists in the autumn of 1945 primarily represented a protest against the politics of accommodation and admiration of their 'patriotic' efforts and active resistance during the war. This admiration nevertheless failed to last beyond the summer of liberation in 1945.

The rescue of the Danish Jews can thus be attributed to a combination of determined passive resistance *and* accommodation which marked the occupation years, complemented by lucky timing. Had the attempt to round up the Jews came in November 1942 as it did in Norway, the end result would most probably have been very different. However that may be, the policy of accommodation made it possible to delay the German action to such an extent that the will to resist in Denmark as well as the rest of Europe had increased.

In many respects, Denmark had a good war. This is probably why Danes today want to fight it again, ignoring the results of professional historical research. As such, the debate testifies to the fundamental democratic-populist (or populist-democratic) and anti-elitist nature of Danish political culture. For many years such attitudes were expressed in views about the European Union. Now they have moved to other areas. That is a different history on which I have written elsewhere.[27]

Notes

1 Hans Fredrik Dahl, Hans Kirchhoff, Joachim Lund & Lars-Erik Vaale (eds.), *Danske tilstande: Norske tilstande. Forskelle og ligheder under tysk besættelse 1940–45* (Copenhagen, 2010).

2 Hans Fredrik Dahl & Hans Kirchhoff, 'Besættelse – dansk og norsk', in: Hans Fredrik Dahl, Hans Kirchhoff, Joachim Lund & Lars-Erik Vaale (eds.), *Danske tilstande: Norske tilstande. Forskelle og ligheder under tysk besættelse 1940–45* (Copenhagen, 2010), 9–30.

3 Anne Eriksen & Jón V. Sigurdsson (eds.), *Negotiating Pasts in the Nordic Countries: Interdisciplinary Studies in History and Memory* (Lund, 2008). See also Claus Bryld, 'The Five Accursed Years: Danish Perception and Usage of the Period of the German Occupation, With a Wider View to Norway and Sweden', *Scandinavian Journal of History*, 2007, 32.

4 Hans Kirchhoff, *Augustoprøret 1943: Samarbejdspolitikkens fald, forudsætninger og forløb*, 3 vols. (Copenhagen, 1979).

5 Hans Kirchhoff, *Samarbejde og modstand under besættelsen: En politisk historie* (Odense, 2001), 13–14.

6 Bo Lidegaard, *A Short History of Denmark in the 20th Century* (Copenhagen, 2009).

7 *Den Parlamentariske Kommissions Beretning til Folketinget*, 14 vols. (Copenhagen, 1946–1953).

8 Claus Bryld & Anette Warring, *Besættelsen som kollektiv erindring: Historie- og traditionsforvaltning af krig og besættelse 1945–1997* (Frederiksberg, 1998); Nils Arne Sørensen, 'Danmarkshistoriens vigtigste parentes: Om besættelsestidens virkningshistorie', in: Joachim Lund (ed.), *Partier under pres* (Copenhagen, 2003), 346–368; Henning Poulsen, 'Dansk modstand og tysk politik', *Den*

Jyske Historiker, 1995, 71, 7–18; Henning Poulsen, *Besættelsesårene 1940–1945* (Århus, 2005).

9 *Udgiverselskabet for Danmarks Nyeste Historie* was founded in 1951 in order to publish the political memoirs of the former Minister of Foreign Affairs Peter Munch. Together with excerpts from his diaries, the memoirs were published in eight massive volumes in 1959–1967. In 1961, the Society initiated systematic research of the political history of the occupation. Researchers working under auspices of the Society had privileged, though not unlimited access to the sources in the national archives. Many of the historians who later became famous as the second generation of historians of the occupation thus trained under the supervision of Jørgen Hæstrup.

10 Bryld & Warring 1998.

11 Tony Judt, *Postwar: A History of Europe since 1945* (London, 2005), 41–42.

12 Judt 2005, 46.

13 Poulsen 1995, 17.

14 Kirchhoff 2001, 7.

15 Hans Kirchhoff (ed.), *Sådan valgte de: Syv dobbeltportrætter fra besættelsens tid* (Copenhagen, 2008), 11–12. The 'Danish Freedom Council' (*Frihedsrådet*) was created in September 1943 to coordinate the fight for liberation. The Council intended to unify the many different groups that made up the Danish resistance movement, bringing together representatives from the Communists, Free Denmark, the Danish Unity Party and Ringen. Key members were Børge Houmann, Mogens Fog, Arne Sørensen, Frode Jakobsen, Erling Foss and Aage Schock. Directives from the British Special Operations Executive, SOE, helped in uniting the different groups.

16 The debate has been thoroughly examined in Bryld & Warring 1998 and by Nils Arne Sørensen, 'Narrating the Second World War in Denmark since 1945', *Contemporary European History*, 14, 2005:3, 295–315.

17 Jens Christian Manniche, *Den radikale historikertradition* (Århus, 1981). A second edition is available at <www.historienu.dk>, accessed on 1 December 2010.

18 Peter Rochegune Munch (1870–1948) was a Danish politician and member of parliament for *Det Radikale Venstre* from 1909 to 1945, representing the island of Langeland. He served in several key posts, as minister of home affairs (1909–1910), minister of defence (1913–1920), minister of foreign affairs (1929–1940) and as the Danish delegate to the League of Nations (1920–1938). See P. Munch, *Erindringer 1870–1947*, 8 vols. (Copenhagen, 1959–1967); Viggo Sjøqvist, *Peter Munch: Manden Politikeren Historikeren* (Copenhagen, 1976); Ole Krarup-Pedersen, *Udenrigsminister P. Munchs opfattelse af Danmarks stilling i international politik* (Copenhagen, 1970). In addition to his scholarly works of history and contributions to general histories of Denmark, Munch left a profound mark on many subsequent generations of schoolchildren through his much-read textbooks on world history. The critical expression 'the German course' (*tyskerkursen*) was coined by the polemicist Bjørn Svensson in an eponymous book from 1983.

19 Kirchhoff 2001 and 2008.

20 *Tidehverv* originated as a left-wing reaction among Danish theologians in the 1920s. The movement was against all attempts to turn the Christian message in the Lutheran church into moralist missives. In the 1970s, the movement was taken over (hijacked in the opinion of some former adherents) by pastor Søren Krarup and turned into an anti-immigration and anti-EU movement. In an interesting manoeuvre, this small group has succeeded in formulating an intellectual language for the populist *Dansk Folkeparti* (Danish People's Party). I have analysed the relationship between the party and the intellectual group and their virtual intellectual hegemony since 2001 in Uffe Østergård, 'Kamp om historien – historie som kamp', in Finn Collin & Jan Faye (eds.), *Ideer vi lever på – Humanistisk viden i videnssamfundet* (Copenhagen, 2008), 204–223.

21 Joachim Lund, *Hitlers spisekammer: Danmark og den europæiske nyordning 1940–43* (Copenhagen, 2005).

22 Claus Bundgård Christensen, Joachim Lund, Niels Wium Olesen & Jakob Sørensen, *Danmark besat: Krig og hverdag 1940–45* (Copenhagen, 2005; 3rd edn 2009).

23 Anders Fogh Rasmussen's address at the commemoration at the Naval Academy on 29 August, 2003. The text is available in Danish on the homepage of the Ministry of the State of Denmark (The Prime Minister's Office): Anders Fogh Rasmussen, 'Tale på Søværnets Officersskole 29. august 2003', <www.statsministeriet.dk>, accessed on 1 December 2010. For reactions to the speech and discussion about the policy of cooperation generally, see Henrik Skovgaard Nielsen, 'Besættelsestiden i den offentlige debat – Samarbejdspolitikken: Moralsk svigt?', <www.befrielsen1945.dk>, accessed on 1 December 2010.

24 Lund 2005; Claus Bundgård Christensen, Niels Bo Poulsen & Peter Scharff Smith, *Under Hagekors og Dannebrog: Danskere i Waffen SS 1940–45* (Copenhagen, 1998).

25 Joachim Lund, 'Building Hitler's Europe: Forced Labor in the Danish Construction Business during Word War II', *Business History Review*, 84, 2010.

26 Christensen, Poulsen & Smith 1998.

27 See, for instance, Uffe Østergård, 'Denmark and the New International Politics of Morality and Remembrance', *Danish Foreign Policy Yearbook*, 2005.

CHAPTER 3

A Separate Story?

Interpretations of Finland in the Second World War

Henrik Meinander

The destiny of Finland in the Second World War was both typical and unique. Finland was one of those newborn states in Eastern Europe that was dragged into the war as a consequence of the Hitler–Stalin Pact in August 1939, but while it became involved in the gradually expanding world conflict, Finland was – unlike all other nations in Central and Eastern Europe – able to defend itself and avoid occupation. This had a decisively positive impact on its societal development during the post-war era and paved the way for a sustained understanding that Finland had fought its own defensive war in the middle of this huge conflict. In fact, Finns still tend to describe their participation in the Second World War as three separate wars: the Winter War (1939–1940) and the Continuation War (1941–1944) against the Soviet Union and the Lapland War (1944–1945) against Germany.

Is this interpretation the result of a nationalistic perception of Finnish history, or can one also find other reasons, motives, attitudes and feelings behind such partiality? In the following, I will analyse this phenomenon by focusing on the dominant Finnish understanding of the Second World War and ask how it has changed since the end of the Cold War. I will also discuss how these changes are connected to, and influenced by, recent and contemporary popular interpretations of the war.

We Are Fighting Our Own War!

Before diving into this world of interpretations, discourses and paradigms, it can be useful to know the basic chronology. The Finnish participation in the Second World War began when the Soviet army, in accordance with the secret protocol in the Stalin–Hitler Pact struck in late autumn 1939 invaded Finland. Although the invasion was stopped by the Finns in this Winter War, the Finnish government was forced to sign an extremely disadvantageous peace treaty with Moscow three months later, which made the country even more vulnerable to a new invasion. That same spring, in 1940, Germany occupied Denmark and Norway. This left the Finns with two options: a balancing act between two dictatorships or a military alliance with Germany. The Finnish leadership chose the latter, seeking to win back the lost territories and also to expand further east, while at the same time hoping to throw the Soviet Union off its back. After the German armed forces launched their attack against the Soviet Union in June 1941, the Finnish army began its own offensive toward Eastern Karelia, where it would spend almost three years, waiting in vain 'to shake hands' with their German brothers-in-arms.

Scandinavian and West European countries had expressed sympathy for the Finns during the Winter War, but did not deliver any substantial military support. When the new war broke out in June 1941, the Finnish President Risto Ryti made it clear in his radio speech that the nation had now begun its second defence against the Soviet Union, one that would prove successful given the simultaneous German offensive. The first having been the Winter War, this logically enough was called the Continuation War. As of the autumn of 1941, when speaking to Scandinavia and the Western Allies, President Ryti would claim that Finland was engaged in a separate defensive war of its own. Typically enough, Ryti and his two wartime governments were rather more vague on this issue in their communications with the Germans, who were deeply annoyed at any suggestion that they were not in the same boat. The Germans could accept the idea of a Finnish defensive war as a part of their anti-Bolshevik propaganda, but labelled all claims to a separate Finnish war as false and traitorous.

The notion of a separate Finnish war was not accepted by the Allies, either, who were well-informed of how systematically the Finnish army synchronised its war efforts with the German campaigns. The Finnish government never signed an official pact with Germany nor was it willing to extend its military efforts further than originally agreed, but through its engagement, Finland nevertheless secured German control of the Baltic, which was crucial for the delivery of Swedish iron ore to the German war industry and tied up numerous Soviet divisions on the Finnish front. Because of this, Britain declared war on Finland in December 1941. In the summer of 1944, the Soviet army forced the Finnish troops into a full-scale retreat in Karelia. At the same time, the Allies had opened a second front against Germany in France, which prepared the way for an armistice between Finland, the Soviet Union and Britain in September 1944. Once more, Finland had to surrender substantial territories and let the Soviet army establish a naval base on the south coast. Furthermore, she was forced to pay reparations to the Soviet Union and fulfil a number of other demanding obligations set out in twenty-three articles of the Armistice Treaty.

According to the thirteenth article, the Finnish government was obliged to try and sentence its war criminals. This commitment was not originally understood to point at Finland's wartime government, but gradually the domestic Communists, who had regained their political rights, increased their criticism of the politicians responsible for wartime policies, and demanded a trial. They were increasingly supported by Liberals and left-wing Social Democrats, who had been critical of the Finnish–German alliance during the war. The decisive step toward Finnish War Trials was taken when the victorious Allies in August 1945 decided to place the decision-makers in Germany and its wartime allies on trial. The Finnish trials took place in the winter of 1945–1946, resulting in prison sentences for former President Ryti and seven key politicians in the wartime government 1940–1944.

During these trials, Finland's wartime policy was discussed and debated in public for the first time. But the trials were dictated by political considerations: neither the defence nor the prosecutor played an open hand. The defence had no interest in admitting that the military alliance with Germany had been close and systematic. This would only have served the interests of the Communists and their masters in Moscow, who saw the trials as a way of strengthening their political support in Finland. Risto Ryti, then, stuck to his original declaration that Finland had fought its own defensive war.

Symptomatically, the prosecutor did not allow Ryti to defend his case and refer to the Winter War as the main reason for the Continuation War. Nor could Ryti speak freely about how the military leadership under Commander-in-Chief Gustaf Mannerheim had acted during the German–Finnish war preparation in winter 1940–1941. Mannerheim, Ryti's successor as president and Finland's foremost wartime hero, had to be saved from accusations at all costs. The trial preceedings were thus so heavily restricted that it was like discussing the intrigues of a play without mentioning its first act or main protagonist. Not surprisingly, Ryti and the other jailed politicians were thought patriotic martyrs by most Finns. Their defence speeches at the trials were to constitute the framework for Finland's dominant patriotic narrative of the Second World War throughout the Cold War. Finland had been an innocent victim of the destructive forces that were set free in the autumn of 1939, and it was this, they argued, that had led to the Continuation War and to Finland's co-operation with Germany.[1]

Driftwood or row-boat?

During the first two post-war decades, this interpretation was also defended by Finnish historians, especially by those who had been involved in the Finnish–German war preparations and propaganda. Once the German diplomat Wipert von Blücher had written in his memoirs that Finland had been thrown into the swirl of great power politics like a piece of driftwood carried by a surging stream, the paradigm found a convincing metaphor. But gradually the driftwood theory started to lose its credibility. Wartime politicians and generals began to publish their memoirs in the 1950s, and although they consciously tried to maintain a 'memoir cartel', this literature revealed a number of contradictions that inspired American and British scholars to dig deeper.[2] In 1957, the American historian

Leonard Lundin published *Finland in the Second World War*, drawing on the memoirs and documents from the Nuremberg and Helsinki trials. Lundin spelt out that Finnish–German wartime cooperation had been a deliberate choice, which had subsequently been denied because of its complex nature and grave consequences. He also openly criticised his Finnish colleagues for their unwillingness to do their job in revealing the true character of Finland's wartime policy.[3]

Finnish scholars replied with a rare sharpness. In 1961, their spokesman Arvi Korhonen published a book with a list of arguments why Finland had to be understood as a victim of the harsh circumstances of war. But Lundin was soon followed by other foreign scholars with even more convincing sources, including the major study in 1967 by the American historian Hans Peter Krosby. His *Suomen valinta 1941* ('Finland's choice in 1941') seriously forced the Finnish scholars to re-evaluate their interpretations. The reluctance openly to analyse the Finnish–German military alliance was by now fading, resulting in numerous academic dissertations and other detailed studies.[4]

However, some influential historians would continue to point out the limits of the Finnish–German alliance, holding on to the claim of a separate Finnish war. They even introduced a new metaphor for this purpose: rather than a piece of lifeless driftwood, Finland had been a skilfully steered row-boat. Nevertheless, by the early 1980s, new research had shown the obvious shortcomings of this metaphor as well.[5] And so the paradigm had shifted away from the historian's established patriotic narrative of a solitary Finnish war. In 1987, Arvi Korhonen's pupil Mauno Jokipii published his monumental work *Jatkosodan synty* ('The Origins of the Continuation War'), questioning and deconstructing both the driftwood theory and the notion of a row-boat. Both theories had by now lost most of their attraction to Finnish historians.[6]

Perhaps more than in any other European country, historians in Finland played a crucial role in the construction of national identity between the mid nineteenth and mid twentieth centuries. Some of them continued to produce syntheses of national historical turning-points even after this, and up until the 1960s their interpretations had a relatively strong impact on popular views on the national past.

But their contributions inevitably lost ground when the printed word was replaced by television and then by the Internet as the dominant media for public debate. As a consequence, what historians said had little impact on public opinion or the political establishment, which continued to believe in, or at the very least feel, an emotional attachment to the notion of a separate Finnish war.

This is something that I, too, have seen as a writer of three general works on Finnish history, in which I tried to articulate Finland's dependency on German military support in the Continuation War,[7] for little of the coverage in the media focused on the key question of Finnish wartime developments. In other words, historians have their own agendas, and so do the media and public opinion. The older generation had obviously been drilled to think in terms of Finland fighting its own war. This was what they had heard President Ryti proclaim in the summer of 1941 and testify during the War Trials. Above all, this is also how Finns have been taught at school and university to look at their national history – a long chain of heroic and lonely defensive wars against Russia.

The Finnish people had experienced similar wars, and their conceptualisation, twice earlier. As an eastern part of the Swedish kingdom, Finland had been occupied by Russian troops in 1808–1809, smoothly transforming into an autonomous Grand Duchy within the Russian empire. This was by no means a tragedy. It turned out to be the starting-point for Finland's development into an independent nation-state. The upshot is that Finns still conceive of this peripheral chain reaction of the Napoleonic Wars as their own war, namely the Finnish War. One hundred years later, in the winter of 1917–1918, the Grand Duchy of Finland was shaken by the societal chaos that the Great War had caused in the Russian empire. When the Bolsheviks took power in Petrograd, the Finns declared themselves independent, but were soon thrown back into conflict once revolution reached Finland. Finland's Reds were supported by the Russian Bolsheviks, but in the face of a military intervention by the German army, the Whites won on this marginal battlefield of the First World War and coined the term the War of Independence to describe it. Since the 1960s, most Finns have remembered it more neutrally as the Civil War.[8]

The impression that Finland fought its 'own' wars was further enforced by the experiences of the Winter War. And even if Finland could not have escaped Soviet occupation without military support from Germany in 1941–1944, this substantial help has until now often been characterised in general narratives as an isolated and peripheral phenomenon in the greater war that Germany was simultaneously fighting. In other words, Finns are inclined to look at their involvement in European military conflicts as separate stories.[9]

Political Motives

The dominant patriotic narrative of Finland's separate wars was not accepted by all Finns, however. Among the Finnish Communists and other left-wing radicals, the bourgeois Finnish government had since 1918 regularly been described as a chauvinistic German satellite state. The Winter War clearly did not fit into this characterisation. But when the Finnish–German military alliance took shape, the accusation seemed more accurate than ever and was fervently supported by Soviet war propaganda.

Finnish Communists were forbidden by law to participate in political life between 1930 and 1944. Their leaders were either in the Soviet Union, imprisoned or gone underground during the war. Once they had returned to public life in the autumn of 1944, they were more than keen to demand a cleansing of all 'Fascists' from the state administration and a thorough rewriting of Finnish history, including Finland's involvement in the Second World War. Their campaign for a Finnish War Trial was part of such rewriting of the past. For them, the trials and the sentences passed were more than justified, and they were intensely critical of the testimony of Ryti and other wartime politicians on trial. For the same reason, the Communists and other left-wing Socialists were explicit in their assessment of the dominant patriotic narrative of a 'separate Finnish war' in 1941–1944. They welcomed the critical contributions on this issue by American and British historians and continued closely to follow and discuss new research findings throughout the Cold War that revealed the systematic nature of Finnish–German co-operation. During the 1960s and 1970s this critical view of the war was shared not only by the radical student movement but also by many pacifists.[10]

The leftist hostility to the separate war theory made it difficult for many others to express their own objections to this chapter of the dominant patriotic narrative. If it were admitted that the Communists, student radicals and pacifists were correct on this historical issue, people might begin to think that their political views and demands were convincing in general terms, too. Such a reaction was clearly not in the interests of wartime policies' moderate critics among liberals and social democrats, even if some of them had already during the war questioned the claim of a separate Finnish war and had remained sceptical toward military co-operation with Germany. Come the 1960s, precious few of them would support the student radicals and pacifists in the debate on the war, especially after the war veterans had been accused of murder by some of the activists.

A reasonably large number of the old wartime critics had been parliamentarians of the small Swedish People's Party, whose political preferences had led them to sympathise with the Western Allies. But more importantly, the so-called peace opposition had also attracted politicians from the big parties, the Social Democrats and the Agrarian League, who had swiftly won leading positions in post-war government and administration.[11] The key figure among them was the Agrarian parliamentarian Urho Kekkonen, who in the autumn of 1944 became minister of justice in the new government and was thereby made responsible for the arrangements of the War Trials. Kekkonen did his job well, indeed too well according to his opponents, who were quick to label him an opportunist and traitor. During the next decade, they would often insinuate that he had actively driven the War Trials in order to earn support from Moscow for his political career. And it was an unquestionably successful career for twenty-five years (1956–1981) as head of state. In the 1950s and early 1960s his opponents drove a number of archetypal smear campaigns against Kekkonen, branding him by turns a drinker, womaniser and Soviet agent. A book about the War Trials published two months before the presidential election in 1956 incriminated Kekkonen for his actions in connection with the trials. The heroes of the book were equally easily identified, namely, Risto Ryti and the seven other convicted politicians. The writer also stood firm in his interpretation that Finland had fought a separate and thus fully honourable war in 1941–1944.[12]

All this created a political undercurrent in the debate about Finnish participation in the Second World War that would last until the 1980s, when Kekkonen retired and the Communists were marginalised in domestic politics. Put differently, the public references to the origin and nature of the Finnish–German military alliance in 1941–1944 was never only or even predominantly a historical discourse. There was also a continuous debate about how Soviet relations and Finnish foreign policy should be handled and who therefore ought to be in power. Kekkonen and his supporters – Communists among them in questions of state affairs – regularly compared their domestic rivals with the conservative politicians in the 1930s, whom they accused of having been both foolish and stubborn in their strong anti-Soviet views.

As head of state, Kekkonen usually preferred to avoid challenging the established truth of the patriotic narrative. A famous exception was a speech he gave in the autumn of 1974, when he openly questioned claims that Finland had drifted into the war in 1941 and had fought it separately from Germany. Kekkonen's interpretation raised protests in the media and inspired the well-known columnist Simo Juntunen in the daily *Suomen Sosialidemokraatti* ('The Social Democrat of Finland') to write tartly: 'I do not know if the President's attempts to rewrite the history of Finland are depressive or pitiful. [...] Or are we paying our oil bill by selling our history?' The sarcasm was too much for Kekkonen who had been a leading architect since the 1950s of the Finnish–Soviet trade agreements, which secured a steady flow of Soviet oil to Finland. The President took his revenge by forcing the chief editor of *Suomen Sosialidemokraatti* to sack Juntunen.

From then on, Kekkonen avoided expressing any explicit interviews on this matter in public. Nevertheless, he would continue to condemn Finnish foreign policy of the 1930s as short-sighted, implying that its consequences had been grave. This irritated his opponents and helped in fact conserve the notion of a separate war in the right-wing media and public discourse in general. It also proved an ideologically handy explanation for many Social Democrats, who since the Second World War had been forced to explain why their party had remained in the wartime governments despite the military alliance with Germany.[13]

Necessary Sacrifices

In other words, behind the more or less vaguely established idea of Finland fighting its own wars was a number of interrelated, disparate and contradictory conceptions of how poorly history had treated Finland. But the notion was maintained not only because it was dictated by political motives or because it fitted so well into the nationalist interpretation of events up until 1939. It tied in equally smoothly with the nationalist interpretation of how Finland had advanced as a society since 1945. As such, and suitably adjusted, it could be used as a logical lead-up to Finnish foreign policy during the Cold War.

By the end of the 1950s Finland had recovered substantially from the material and human losses of the war. A swift industrialisation and urbanisation followed, which transformed Finland into a welfare state with almost as generous social security as in the other Nordic states. This was certainly something to be proud of, not least when one thought back to the difficult times during and immediately after the Second World War. The war effort and losses were increasingly described as necessary sacrifices in aid of the common good, embodied the welfare state and a stable foreign policy.

The war thus gradually turned into one of the four main chapters in Finland's national history. The creation of the Finnish nation-state had already been established as the first two chapters, whereas the construction of the welfare state would equally self-evidently become the fourth and thus far the last chapter in this patriotic narrative. But when talking about the struggle for national survival, nothing can challenge the narrative of Finland in the Second World War. It follows that the whole epoch has been understood as the test of great manhood in Finnish collective memory. Not surprisingly, such a heroic status in the national history has safeguarded the popular notion that the Finnish participation in the war was a separate defensive war. This has been especially evident in connection with public commemorations of the war, which reach their annual peak on Independence Day on 6 December.[14]

However, in foreign affairs it was not necessarily advisable to pronounce the separate nature of the Finnish participation in the war. Until the 1960s, the Finnish leadership's focus was on stabilising the relationship with the Soviet Union, which decreed in the Paris Peace Treaty of 1947 that Finland had been a German ally. Public claims of a separate war or too explicit a defence of wartime policy could thus not be a part of the Finnish agenda. Once Finland had gained a stronger position as a non-allied, neutral state, this eloquent silence was occasionally broken by a more self-reliant interpretation of Finnish wartime policy. One of the most telling came from the influential Finnish diplomat Max Jakobson, who in his 1968 book on Finnish foreign policy argued that the decisions taken in 1941 proved that Finland was already then being led by politicians who understood the necessity of a proactive foreign policy.[15]

During the presidency of Kekkonen's successor Mauno Koivisto (1982–1994), a more outspoken apologetic interpretation of Finland's wartime policy, including hints of a separate war, took shape in official diplomacy and other foreign policy declarations. What lay behind the changing attitude was clearly the *glasnost* (openness) campaign in the Soviet Union, which reactivated old views on the war among leading politicians and diplomats. After the Soviet empire had collapsed and Finland had joined the European Union in 1995, this trend was further strengthened. State officials took to stating that the Finnish involvement in the war had been an unavoidable and necessary struggle for national existence.

One of these outspoken statesmen was Mauno Koivisto. Starting in the last years of his presidency, Koivisto – a decorated war veteran himself – touched on wartime issues from many angles in his books and public speeches. His personal war experiences were clearly one important reason for his popularity and crushing victories in the presidential elections in 1982 and 1988. It was also a further reason why his interpretations of Finnish participation in the war were especially noted, not least when he defended as correct and clever the wartime decisions by his presidential predecessors Risto Ryti and Gustaf Mannerheim. While this was not an explicit comment on whether Finland had fought its own, separate war, it was no doubt easily understood as such. It therefore gave a further boost to the deeply rooted notion of Finnish history as a chain of lonely wars against Russia.[16]

Koivisto's successors as president, Martti Ahtisaari (1994–2000) and Tarja Halonen (from 2000), have so far been less reticent about Finland at war. Ahtisaari was born in 1937 in the Karelian harbour town of Viipuri and was one of almost half a million evacuated Finns who lost their homes in the war. He often referred to these childhood memories in his public speeches, most noticeably when he received the Nobel Peace Prize in Oslo in 2008. He took the opportunity to explain the emotional motivation for his lifetime commitment to humanitarianism and peace. Such personal reflections cannot be understood as an open political statement about Finland's participation in the war, but they have been taken as a reminder of the Finnish civilians' severe suffering. It is not difficult to read this as implying that wartime Finland was more of a victim than an aggressor.[17]

In contrast to these indirect statements by Koivisto and Ahtisaari, President Tarja Halonen has twice publically declared that Finland fought a separate war. The first occasion was a speech on Finnish foreign policy delivered in France in March 2005. Finnish wartime history was not the issue of her presentation, and it was in fact touched on in one single sentence only, in which she declared: 'For us the Second World War meant a separate war against the Soviet Union; the Finns did not put themselves in debt for this to others.' The Russian Ministry of Foreign Affairs reacted immediately by reminding that Finland had signed the Paris Peace Treaty in 1947, where Finland was plainly declared one of the German allies. Tarja Halonen did not reply to this criticism, but repeated in the autumn of 2008 in a public seminar on wartime memories that she still preferred to understand the Finnish struggle as a separate war: 'I was criticised both at home and even more so abroad. But I claim that the speech reflected and still reflects how the Finns feel about the issue.'[18]

It would be far-fetched to read these short statements as a decisive change in the official understanding of wartime history. President Halonen did not present a coherent analysis of Finnish history. Furthermore, a constitutional reform in 2000 had made her status in the Finnish political system much weaker than that of her predecessors. This clearly rendered presidential statements less significant. Her reflections on the issue rather show that the Finnish participation in the Second World War is no longer a crucial issue in Finnish foreign policy. As an established EU country, the Finnish government focuses much more on current questions, such as the Lisbon Treaty and its article on common defence obligations. President Halonen's thoughts about the war should therefore be understood more as a politically appropriate response to popular expectations and trends in the memory culture on Finnish wartime history.

A Defensive Victory

Before analysing a new wave of interpretations of wartime developments, it is important to point out that the popular commemoration of the war was never particularly discouraged in Finland during the Cold War. Finland was the only combatant nation that systematically repatriated the bodies of its fallen, buried them in their local churchyards, and soon after the war erected monuments in each of these so-called heroes' graveyards, which became core sites for a collective cult of death and commemoration of the sacrifice in more general terms. As the deepest war wounds healed in the 1950s, a wide range of domestic war literature came out, first traditional combat and regimental memoirs by war veterans, then fiction of various kinds, and finally a collection of academic studies.[19]

The most famous of these war impressions was without question Väinö Linna's epic novel *Tuntematon sotilas* ('Unknown Soldier'), published in 1954, which depicted both the harsh reality and raucous experiences of Finland's soldiers by following the fate of a machine gun company during the Continuation War. The novel became an all-time best-seller and was made into an equally popular film. Together, the novel and the film have had a decisive impact on the popular perception of the war. The key political message was that the infantry privates had done their duty even if they had neither really admired Mannerheim nor been unaware of the Finnish dependency on the military alliance with Germany. Despite all the suffering and loss, the men had crucially understood that post-Winter War Finland lacked any realistic alternatives.[20]

It is not an exaggeration to say that this interpretation was deeply rooted in a popular sentiment which not only survived but even ruled supreme throughout the Cold War. It could be read and understood in different ways, and this was its strength. It could be construed both as a burlesque tribute to the notion of a separate Finnish war and as sullen grassroots critique of the bourgeois society that the soldiers had been sent out to defend. Never ruled out as war propaganda by the student and pacifist movements, the novel had by the end of the Cold War reached an undisputed position as *the* Finnish war story. It thus ousted the war epic *Fänrik Ståls sägner* ('The Tales of Ensign Stål') on the Finnish War of 1808–1809, which had functioned as a cornerstone in the ideological construction of Finland since the late 1840s.[21]

Not surprisingly, the collapse of the Soviet empire brought to the surface a mixture of feelings, themes and questions in Finland which for different reasons had been forgotten, denied or consciously hidden during the Cold War. Among the first visible reactions were the demands that Russia ought to return the ceded territories in Karelia that had been handed over to the Soviet Union in the Armistice and Peace Treaties. In 1944, no sensible person could have argued that Finland had been victorious in the conflict. Ten years later, when Väinö Linna hinted at the question at the end of *Tuntematon sotilas* he let the joker of the company laugh that 'The Union of the Soviet Socialist Republics won, but plucky little Finland came second'. After the Soviet Union had been disbanded, some went as far as claiming that the Soviet dissolution was in fact proof of Finland's victory in the conflict and thereby evidence of Finland's entitlement to Karelia. The campaign was supported by some influential exiled Karelians and their cultural heritage organisations, but never won large popular support or any substantial political backing.[22]

Another outcome of the Soviet collapse was a rather short but vigorous renaissance of the remembrance of many of those political right-wing and paramilitary organisations that had been forbidden in 1944. A more lasting phenomenon has been a renewed and partly transformed interest in Mannerheim, who had lost some of his heroic aura during the Cold War over some political disputes about his role as commander-in-chief in all the wars Finland had been involved in between 1918 and 1945. The traditional Mannerheim cult, which has been an established part of Finnish military culture and many state ceremonials since the 1930s, was now seen in a more positive light and gained in publicity. In addition, Mannerheim mobilised a new set of admirers, both among various domestic right-wing groups and in bourgeois Russia, where his thirty-year career in the imperial army has become a source of nostalgia for a pre-revolutionary society. The new Mannerheim cult is clearly ignorant of the critical discourse and historical evidence of his military decisions in general and of his crucial role in the Finnish–German alliance in 1941–1944 in particular. It was as if the fall of the Soviet Union had made it possible to return to the official wartime image of Mannerheim.[23]

The Finnish devotion to Mannerheim has much in common with the heroic mythology born around many other famous European statesmen such as Churchill and de Gaulle. And yet there is something special about how many down-to-earth Finns still rate the cosmopolitan and in many senses the Swedish-Russian elite figure of Mannerheim as their national hero number one. One explanation is that they understand Mannerheim as the proud figurehead of their struggle to maintain Western civilisation in Finland. While he did serve three decades as a military officer in imperial Russia, that was during an era when Russia was more than ever connected to, and influenced by, Western civilisation. During the Cold War it was less wise to say in public how outspokenly and fiercely anti-Bolshevik Mannerheim had been during his career in Finland. As the British scholar John Screen so convincingly argued in his biography of the Marshal of Finland, this antipathy was in fact the guiding light in Mannerheim's life's work from 1917 onward.[24]

A parallel trend in the popular wartime discourse has been a return to a narrower and sometimes openly nationalistic view on Finnish participation in the Second World War. The international context of the war has either been set aside or handled with a nationalist pathos, which has resulted in a common overestimation of the domestic role in the war and a renewed circulation of the notion of a separate Finnish war. The most spectacular manifestations were the many films and exhibitions about the war era, which either omitted to mention or only obscurely hinted at the substantial military support from, and dependency on, Germany. A case in point is the state-aided remembrance culture of the defensive struggle at the Karelian Isthmus in the summer of 1944, when a large-scale Soviet offensive was after two weeks of rapid retreat stopped at Tali-Ihantala largely thanks to efficient German support. This battle is still commonly known as a purely national struggle for survival and for the same reason is widely remembered as the great Defensive Victory in Finnish history.[25]

It is not a coincidence that such memory production around Tali-Ihantala has many similarities with the current phenomena in the Baltic states and other parts of the 'new Europe'. During the Cold War, all these East European countries were in one way or another forced to censor or deny their nationalist and anti-Soviet feelings and memories connected with their experiences of the Second World War. Once the restrictions were lifted, the reactions proved – not surprisingly – rather forceful. However, it is equally obvious that the Finnish debate has in other respects differed considerably from the Baltic and other East European discourses about the war. Gradually distancing themselves from the nationalist paradigm, Finnish historians have systematically begun to highlight the depth nature of the Finnish–German bonds between 1941 and 1944. Such developments are yet to take place among historians in other parts of Eastern Europe. And even if these documented findings are still regularly ignored by Finnish popular opinion, they have moderated the views of the leading intellectuals and politicians, who significantly have seldom advocated a restoration of Karelia or a rehabilitation of the eight wartime politicians convicted in the Finnish War Trials in 1946.

The Moral Turn

Does this suggest that the pattern of the discourse among Finnish academics during the last two decades has born a closer resemblance to the West European template? Yes and no. In principle, the Finnish deconstruction of the nationalist paradigm has followed the same route as in Scandinavia and many other parts of Western Europe. At the same time, Finnish historians are now reasonably receptive to new ways of analysing the history of the war. This has resulted in a number of studies inspired by micro-history, new cultural history, the history of the senses and even postmodern history, all of which have contributed to 'the new war history'.

Nonetheless, the two trends do not necessarily go hand in hand. Deconstructions of the nationalist paradigm are hardly possible without comparative and other macro analyses of the phenomenon, which put it in a larger context and uncover its imagined national framework. Recently published Finnish studies on wartime history give the impression of an unintended so-called methodological nationalism. The so-called new war history research has, for example, so far not shed much light on why and how Finland became involved in the Second World War. It points out the blind spots of traditional military history without advancing its own contextual explanations of the process.[26]

In defence of the new war history it has to be said that its outspoken aim has never been the introduction of new macro theories. Quite the opposite, much of the new cultural historical research is utterly sceptical of, or at least uninterested in, such attempts. The outcome of this genre of research has been a swiftly expanding field of increasingly disparate topics and research perspectives, which are often chosen for what should be characterised as postmodern purposes. Almost every wartime social class and age group, nearly every ethnic and sexual minority is now scrutinised separately, which inevitably brings to mind Keith Jenkins' postmodern claim about history writing in general: 'In that sense all classes/groups write their collective autobiographies.'[27] The consequence has been a growing ignorance of the structural forces in international politics and warfare. And from this follows difficulties in finding a common platform for a discourse on wartime history even within the academic community.

An important exception to this rule was a state-funded research project in 2004–2008 about the Soviet prisoners of war (POWs) and interned Soviet civilians, which examined in close detail the high death rates in the Finnish camps in the winter of 1941–1942 and the transfers to the German authorities. The project was initiated by President Tarja Halonen in response to international reactions to a controversial book on the topic by the Finnish journalist Elina Sana, who claimed that the Finnish authorities had been anti-Semitic and deliberately picked out Jewish prisoners for the transfers of POWs to the Germans. The research project found convincing evidence that the Finnish authorities could not be accused of any substantial anti-Semitic tendencies in this exchange of prisoners with Germany. A total of 2,916 POWs were transferred to the Germans and only 52 were classified in the official documents as Jews. However, the project reports also revealed that the stunningly high death rates at the Finnish camps (30.3 per cent) were not caused only by food shortages but also by poor administration and inadequate food distribution.[28]

This is as far as the Finnish state has gone to organise and finance large-scale investigations of morally controversial issues in Finnish participation in the war. Various public demands for truth and reconciliation commissions about the war have naturally been heard in Finland, too, over the years, but so far the government has played them down by pronouncing the importance of an independent research agenda. This stance was last confirmed in March 2010 when the Ministry of Justice went public with an inquiry that pointed out a number of legal weaknesses in the Finnish War Trials in 1945–1946. The inquiry was a reply to public demands for a posthumous rehabilitation of the eight leading politicians imprisoned for their wartime decisions. The government declared that the demands were indeed morally understandable, but rejected them and recommended that the debate should continue without any further interference from the state apparatus.[29]

Why did the Finnish government then not follow this principle in the question of the Soviet POWs? The driving force behind this large state-funded research project was the international discourse on the Holocaust, which reached the Nordic countries, too, after some delay. The first empirical studies of Finnish wartime attitudes toward, and responsibility for, the Holocaust were published in the 1980s, but they revealed nothing spectacular or aggravating, rather the opposite. While they did return eight Jewish refugees to the Germans, the Finnish government had refused to hand over its own Jewish citizens. Some Finnish historians have referred to these findings as evidence of a distinct Finnish agenda throughout the Continuation War, which would motivate its characterisation of a separate Finnish war. However, in 2008 Oula Silvennoinen revealed in his doctoral thesis on the co-operation between Finnish and German security police that some members of the Finnish police had in 1942 been involved in the mass murder of Communists and Jews among the Soviet POWs in German-controlled northern Finland. His findings were much publicised and by many were understood as evidence of the closeness of the Finnish–German alliance.[30]

Some have even drawn the conclusion that the Finnish–German alliance had a hidden anti-Semitic programme and that Finland was thus partly to blame for the Holocaust. Academic historians have so far shied away from such far-reaching conclusions, although many have shown that only a few Finns expressed their disgust in public at the treatment of the Jewish population in German-occupied Europe. The most common explanation to this indifference toward the Jewish victims is that the Finnish state and its citizens were forced to prioritise their own struggle for national survival, and were unaware of the total figures of the mass destruction of Jews and other victims of this systematic terror.

I touched upon this issue in a recent book on Finnish society in 1944 and came to the same conclusion as Tony Judt, whose analysis of the Holocaust discourse shows that there were only two groups in wartime Europe who understood the ongoing war as a project to destroy the Jews: 'It was the Nazis and the Jews themselves'. This is clearly a challenge for historians, who are now asked to comment on public discourses in which the Holocaust is without hesitation understood as the main chapter of wartime history. Judt points out that the growing emphasis on the Holocaust is a Western European and American phenomenon. On the eastern side of the Oder–Neisse-line, many academics and intellectuals are annoyed at such a delimitation of the discourse. Their question is why all the other Eastern European victims – and there were even more of them – are denied such posthumous rehabilitation.[31]

It is obvious that the public discourses in Denmark, Norway and Sweden have to a great extent followed the same paths during the last fifteen years as the West European discourse about the Holocaust. Each of the three countries has a state-funded centre for Holocaust studies and remembrance, which have spread information about European genocide and stimulated discussion about their own national responsibility for the Holocaust. In Sweden, a large research project on the issue has resulted in studies and anthologies debating in detail the Western European discourse and 'moral turn'.[32]

The Finnish Holocaust discourse has so far differed markedly from the Nordic pattern, partly perhaps there is traditionally a delay in the Finnish reception of international ideas and views. However, a more obvious reason seems to be that Finnish wartime experiences are in some crucial respects more like those in Eastern Europe than in the western parts of German-occupied Europe. The substantial human and territorial losses have together with personal memories of the war played such a dominant role in research and public discourse that the idea of a Finnish Holocaust centre could easily be seen as a bad joke. Another, more unique reason for the Finnish reluctance to participate in this 'Holocaustification' of the Second World War is that Finnish Jews did their patriotic duty, fully taking part in the war despite the military alliance with Germany in 1941–1944. How can such an existential choice be explained in a museum exhibition intended for teenagers and American tourists?

Typically enough, the only new war remembrance project that Finnish politicians have recently promoted is a museum highlighting the battle of Tali-Ihantala on the Karelian Isthmus in the summer of 1944. This also explains why the public reaction to some of the recent journalistic accusations of Finnish responsibility for the Holocaust have been so emotional. Like many other people in the eastern half of Europe, Finns have in their commemorations of the war thus far focused mainly on the consequences for their own nation.

Concluding Remarks

How long will this popular attitude last? Few historians today have any illusions about their impact on popular perceptions of the war. In other words, in the future the dominant view on wartime Finland will presumably continue to be directed much more by societal development and ideological atmosphere than by academic discoveries and discourses. It is possible that in the face of an ongoing fragmentation of research and of wartime memories, the story of Finland in the Second World War will gradually lose its status as the main chapter in the patriotic narrative. Such signs are already clearly visible and may grow even stronger if Finnish society is incapable of finding effective solutions to all the structural problems that the worldwide financial crisis has further deepened. In this sense the future of wartime memories appears to depend on the destiny of the Finnish welfare state and its European frameworks.

Another safe guess is that the mental gap between popular perceptions and scholarly discourses will continue to widen. Professional historians today face a number of challenges within their own discipline, which make it increasingly difficult to gather the knowledge of wartime history into contextual analyses and transparent debates. One of these challenges is the more or less unconscious – and growing – postmodernist tendency in history writing which may well within a few decades split the discipline into a number of new branches with their own agendas and vocabularies.

Notes

1 Henrik Meinander, 'Kriget, ansvaret och historiens domstol. Krigsansvarighetsdomstolens historiografi', *Historisk Tidskrift för Finland*, 1996:2, 191–220; Henrik Meinander, *Suomi kansalaissodasta 2000-luvulle* (Espoo, 1999), 131–269.

2 Von Blücher's memoirs were soon followed by a number of prestigious Finnish memoirs and biographies: Gustaf Mannerheim, *Minnen*, 2 vols. (Helsinki, 1951–1952); Väinö Tanner, *Suomen tie rauhaan 1943–1944* (Helsinki, 1952); Erik Heinrichs, *Mannerheim-gestalten*, 2 vols. (Helsinki, 1957–1959).

3 Wipert von Blücher, *Ödesdigra år: Diplomatiska minnen från Finland 1935–1944* (Helsinki, 1950); C. Leonard Lundin, *Finland in the Second World War* (Indiana, 1957).

4 Arvi Korhonen, *Barbarossa-suunnitelma ja Suomi: Jatkosodan synty* (Porvoo, 1961); Anthony Upton, *Finland in Crisis 1940–1941: A Study in Small-state Politics* (London, 1964); Hans Peter Krosby, *Suomen valinta 1941* (Helsinki, 1967).

5 Jukka Tarkka, *13. artikla: Suomen sotasyyllisyyskysymys ja liittoutuneiden sotarikospolitiikka vuosina 1944–1946* (Helsinki, 1977); Ohto Manninen, *Toteutumaton valtioliitto: Suomi ja Ruotsi talvisodan jälkeen* (Helsinki, 1977); Ohto Manninen, *Suur-Suomen ääriviivat* (Helsinki, 1980); Antti Laine, *Suur-Suomen kahdet kasvot: Itä-Karjalan siviiliväestön asema suomalaisessa miehityshallinnossa 1941–1944* (Helsinki, 1982).

6 Mauno Jokipii, *Jatkosodan synty: Tutkimuksia Saksan ja Suomen sotilaallisesta yhteistyöstä 1940–41* (Helsinki, 1987). Among recently published studies, see Markku Jokisipilä, *Aseveljiä vai liittolaisia?: Suomi, Saksa ja Ryti–Ribbentrop-sopimus* (Helsinki, 2004); Jari Leskinen et al., 'Uhri vai hyökkääjä? Jatkosodan synty historiankirjoituksen kuvaamana', in: Jari Leskinen & Antti Juutilainen (eds.), *Jatkosodan pikkujättiläinen* (Helsinki, 2005), 38–44.

7 Henrik Meinander, *Tasavallan tiellä: Suomi kansalaissodasta 2000-luvulle* (Espoo, 1999); Henrik Meinander, *Finlands historia: Linjer, strukturer, vändpunkter* (Helsinki, 2006); Henrik Meinander, *Finland 1944: Krig, samhälle, känslolandskap* (Helsinki, 2009).

8 Max Engman, *Ett långt farväl: Finland mellan Sverige och Finland efter 1809* (Stockholm, 2009), 70–145; Meinander 1999, 16–24.

9 See, for example, Seppo Myllyniemi, *Suomi sodassa 1939–1945* (Helsinki, 1982); Leskinen et al. 2005.

10 Ilkka Herlin, 'Suomi-neidon menetetty kunnia: Ajopuuteorian historiografiaa', in Päiviö Tommila (ed.), *Historiantutkijan muotokuva* (Helsinki, 1998), 201–214.

11 Henrik Meinander, 'Kekkonen och Sfp: Några episoder och personrelationer', in Siv Sandberg (ed.), *Svenska folkpartiet genom 100 år* (Helsinki, 2006), 153–172.

12 Yrjö Soini, *Kuin Pietari hiilivalkealla: Sotasyyllisyysasian vaiheet 1945–1949* (Helsinki, 1956); Meinander 1996, 196–216.

13 Antero Jyränki, *Kolme vuotta linnassa: Muistiinpanoja ja jälkiviisauksia* (Porvoo, 1990), 121–124; Sami Sinervo, 'Ajopuuteoria – kirjallista asevelvollisuutta', *Helsingin Sanomat*, 20 June 1991.

14 Meinander 2009, 392–398.

15 Max Jakobson, *Kuumalla linjalla: Suomen ulkopolitiikan ydinkysymyksiä 1944–1968* (Helsinki, 1968), 35.

16 Mauno Koivisto, *Ung soldat: Från skolbänken till skyttegraven* (Stockholm, 2001); Mauno Koivisto, *Itsenäiseksi imperiumin kainalossa: Mietteitä kansojen kohtaloista* (Helsinki, 2004).

17 <http://nobelprize.org/nobel_prizes/peace/laureates/2008/ahtisaari-lecture.html> accessed on 1 December 2010.

18 <http://yle.fi/aohjelmat/apiste/arkisto/id15552.html> accessed on 1 December 2010; Henrik Meinander, 'Förvånande fadäs', *Hufvudstadsbladet*, 13

March 2005 available at <http://www.mtv3.fi/uutiset/kotimaa.shtml/arkistot/kotimaa/2008/11/752198> accessed on 1 December 2010.

19 Henrik Meinander, 'Andra världskriget i finländsk historiekultur', in: Claus B. Christensen & Anette Warring (eds.), *Finland og Danmark: Krig og Besættelse* (Roskilde, 2007), 12–19.

20 Väinö Linna, *Tuntematon sotilas* (Helsinki, 1954); Väinö Linna, *Unknown Soldier* (London, 1957).

21 The novel was a commercial success from the start, but was initially scorned by some reviewers and commentators. Right-wing journalists and academics blamed the writer for smearing Finnish officers and female help brigades (Lotta Svärd), while some Communists again accused Linna of a badly disguised revanchist attitude. See Yrjö Varpio, *Väinö Linnan elämä* (Helsinki, 2006), 320–367, 486–514.

22 Pentti Virrankoski, *Karjala takaisin – suhteet Venäjään terveiksi* (Lappeenranta, 1994).

23 Leonid Vlasov, *Mannerheim Pietarissa 1887–1904* (Helsinki, 1994); Henrik Meinander, 'Mitä Jägerskiöld tähän sanoisi! Poimintoja itsenäisyysaikaa koskevasta Mannerheim-tutkimuksesta', in: Henrik Meinander (ed.) *Scripta Mannerheimiana: Puheenvuoroja Mannerheim-kirjallisuudesta & valikoiva bibliografia* (Helsinki, 1996), 69–82.

24 J. E. O. Screen, *Mannerheim: The Finnish Years* (London, 2000).

25 Typical examples include the multimedia presentation *Ihantalan ihme* (the Miracle of Ihantala) at the Artillery Museum in Hämeenlinna <http://www.tykistomuseo.fi/nayttelyt-esitykset/multimediaesitykset/> and the action film *Tali-Ihantala 1944* <http://www.tali-ihantala.fi/nf/> accessed on 1 December 2010.

26 Ville Kivimäki & Tiina Kinnunen (eds.), *Ihminen sodassa: Suomalaisten kokemuksia talvi- ja jatkosodasta* (Helsinki, 2006); Sari Näre & Jenni Kirves (eds.), *Ruma sota: Talvi- ja jatkosodan vaiettu historia* (Helsinki, 2008).

27 Keith Jenkins, *Re-thinking History* (London, 2003), 22.

28 Elina Sana, *Luovutetut: Suomen ihmisluovutukset Gestapolle* (Helsinki, 2003); Lars Westerlund (ed.), *Prisoners of War and People Handed over to Germany and the Soviet Union in 1939–1945* (Helsinki, 2008).

29 <http://www.om.fi/Etusivu/Julkaisut/Selvityksiajaohjeita/Selvitystenjaohjeidenarkisto/Selvityksiajaohjeita2010/1266333593848> accessed on 1 December 2010.

30 Hannu Rautkallio, *Suomen juutalaisten aseveljeys* (Helsinki, 1989); Oula Silvennoinen, *Salaiset aseveljet: Suomen ja Saksan turvallisuuspoliisiyhteistyö 1933–1944* (Helsinki, 2008), 187–260.

31 Tony Judt, 'The Problem of Evil in Postwar Europe', *New York Review of Books*, 14 February 2008; Meinander 2009, 301.

32 Lars M. Andersson & Mattias Tydén (eds.), *Sverige och Nazityskland: Skuldfrågor och moraldebatt* (Stockholm, 2007), 9–25; Johan Östling, *Nazismens sensmoral: Svenska erfarenheter i andra världskrigets efterdyning* (Stockholm, 2008).

CHAPTER 4

'The Beloved War'

The Second World War and the Icelandic National Narrative

Guðmundur Hálfdanarson

In the year 2000, the leading historical journal in Iceland, *Saga* ('History'), ran a whole issue on the course of Icelandic twentieth-century historiography. The editors had asked a number of historians to examine how different periods and fields of Icelandic history had been treated in the academic and popular historical literature in the century that was coming to a close. Reading the twelve contributions, one is struck by the limited amount of attention Icelandic historians have paid to the Second World War and its role in Icelandic history. As a matter of fact, the history of the war barely gets a mention in the volume, except for an article dealing with Icelandic foreign policy and relations with the world. Even there, less than one page is devoted to this crucial period in the history of Iceland.[1]

This does not mean that the Second World War has been ignored in Icelandic historical literature, as its story has been told in numerous popular works and historical surveys of the twentieth century.[2] But it has been mostly absent in historical or political debates, which renders the bibliography on the war in Iceland fairly short. The apparent disinterest is rather surprising, because it is, without doubt, one of the most fateful periods in the history of the country. Unlike much of Europe, Iceland was not devastated by the war – on the contrary, it was a time of rapid economic growth. Moreover, the Second World War thrust the relatively isolated island into modernity and onto the stage of international politics, as the North Atlantic became a centre of attention in the struggle for global hegemony. Finally, the foundation of the Republic of Iceland on 17 June 1944 completed the development toward full statehood, severing administrative ties with Denmark that had lasted for more than five centuries. The obvious question is why a period so important for Iceland's status as a sovereign nation-state has not been at the centre of Icelandic historical research, all the more so as sovereignty has long been regarded as the ultimate goal of Iceland's political development.

The answers have to be sought in a combination of factors. First, one can hardly expect historical research to be as varied and broad in scope in a country such as Iceland, with its very small population, as it is in much larger societies. This has, of course, marked Icelandic historiography, which tends to focus on a fairly narrow range of issues. There is only room for a very few specialists in most fields of historical research. Second, from very early on, Iceland was placed decisively in the Allied camp. Although this did not happen through the conscious policy of the Icelandic government, it freed the Icelandic political and cultural elite from any implications of collaboration or active cooperation with Nazi Germany during the war years. The moral subtext in much of the European (including Nordic) debates on the history of the Second World War has therefore been absent from Iceland, and there has not been the same incentive to revisit the war there as in the neighbouring countries. Finally, the Second World War seems to contradict the general storyline of the Icelandic national narrative. Since the beginning of the so-called struggle for independence in the nineteenth century, historians and political commentators have stressed the adverse effects of foreign rule on both the economy and culture. Only through the full sovereignty of the Icelandic state and the preservation of their national culture, or so the story goes, could Icelanders establish a prosperous society. It has proven difficult to fit the Second World War into this narrative framework, which is why it tends to be seen not as an integral part of Icelandic history in spite of its obvious significance. We therefore need to see the war in its historical context to grasp its place in Iceland's historiography.

Iceland in the Second World War

At the beginning of the Second World War, Iceland had been a sovereign state, united with Denmark under a common king, for just over two decades. Like so many of the small nation-states in Europe, the Icelandic state had been established in the wake of the First World War. This happened through the so-called Act of Union with Denmark, which was negotiated during the early summer of 1918 and came into effect on 1 December that same year.[3] A dual monarchy was established out of the vestiges of the Danish conglomerate monarchy, with the Danish king serving as a monarch for two very unequal parts – the sovereign states of Denmark and Iceland. The Act gave Iceland full control over its domestic affairs, while the Danish king functioned as a figurehead with no real power over the Icelandic government or legislative processes. Authority over Iceland's foreign policy was less clear-cut, however, as the Danish government continued to administer the Icelandic foreign service. According to the Act of Union, Denmark could only act at the behest of the Icelandic government, or 'pour l'Islande,' as it was formulated in all official foreign policy documents pertaining to Icelandic affairs.[4] This meant that Iceland had the authority to develop its own foreign policy, but it lacked – at least during the first years of its sovereignty – the means to implement it.

In the 1920s and 1930s, the Icelandic government showed limited interest in the country's foreign relations, except when it came to issues related to foreign trade. The main precept of Icelandic foreign policy in the inter-war years was to defend the country's declaration of permanent neutrality, which was stated in the Act of Union. The implication was that Iceland had no intention of meddling in the affairs of other states, and expected others to act accordingly when it came to internal Icelandic affairs. This was both a statement of the obvious – that is, as a small and relatively poor state, with no military force, Iceland had no real opportunity to have an impact on the international stage – and a pragmatic decision. The only hope Iceland had of defending itself from foreign aggression was to stay out of international conflicts, while it had to place its trust in others to ward off potential assailants.

From the beginning of the Second World War it was painfully clear that a declaration of neutrality was now utterly meaningless, at least for those who lacked the military means to secure their own defences. In a time of war, as Ólafur Thors, Minister of Economic Affairs, chairman of the centre-right Independence Party, and future Prime Minister of Iceland, pointed out in his 1939 end-of-year address to readers of the conservative daily *Morgunblaðið*, the high and mighty did not hesitate to crush their weaker neighbours. 'Last spring we heard loud groans from Czechoslovakia,' he wrote, and that country 'has now been erased from the map'. Poland had met a similar fate, he continued, while Estonia, Latvia, and Lithuania had bought their right to exist by trading their sovereignty to one of the major European powers, the Soviet Union. Yet another European small state, Finland, was fighting valiantly for its freedom, fending off 'one of the most immoral and despicable assaults in history'. Thors's sad conclusion was that 'we Icelanders remain alone among those who regained their freedom [at the end of the First World War] and it is no wonder that we think about the others, with great sympathy and understanding of their difficult fate'.[5]

These facts were brought home to Iceland on the morning of 10 May 1940 when British warships entered the Reykjavík harbour and British soldiers marched into the heart of the Icelandic capital.[6] The Icelandic government had no choice but to accept the inevitable, surrendering unconditionally to the British occupation. In a radio address to the nation, Prime Minister Hermann Jónasson, a centrist, protested vigorously at what he called a blatant 'violation of Iceland's neutrality and the impairment of its independence' by the British occupation. He reassured his listeners, however, that the British authorities had given their solemn guarantee not to interfere in internal Icelandic affairs and to leave the country as soon as hostilities were over. Jónasson therefore urged all Icelanders 'to treat the British soldiers [...] as guests and to show them, as any other guest, full courtesy in every way'.[7]

From this point on to the end of the war, the actions of the Icelandic authorities can be termed continual negotiation between active participation on the Allied side of the conflict and the desire to stay out of the war. This balancing act characterised both the official discourse of the Icelandic government and comments in the press. Publically, the British forces were resented, because they were seen as a threat to Icelandic identity and to national sovereignty, but in practice the Allied military presence in Iceland was tolerated without much complaint. Iceland in fact profited handsomely from the foreign forces stationed in the country, and had they been asked, the Icelandic authorities and the general public would certainly have confirmed that they preferred British occupation to that by Germans.[8] The only consistent resistance to the British military in Iceland came from the Socialist Unity Party, which claimed that there was absolutely no difference between British and German imperialism. With the British occupation, its party organ *Þjóðviljinn* argued, Icelanders 'had been turned into a target in the bloody conflict between the British and German capitalists fighting over world markets and resources – or into petty change in international negotiations between the capitalist superpowers to be used at the conclusion of the war.'[9] This changed more or less overnight when the Germans invaded the Soviet Union during the summer of 1941. As the Soviet Union entered into the Allied fold, former foes suddenly turned into friends and allies. 'Your fate, your national liberty, your children's future depends on the opponents of Fascism and the victory of the Red Army and other liberating military forces in this war. If they lose, then our freedom is lost, our culture destroyed', declared the editors of *Þjóðviljinn* in 1942, fully embracing the presence of the Allied forces in Iceland. The Second World War had thus been transformed into a war of liberation, at the same time as the victory of 'the united front of the Soviet nations, of the British nation, the United States, and China' had become a necessary prerequisite for Iceland's independence.[10]

From a purely economic point of view, the Second World War was obviously a godsend to Iceland. For this reason, it was often referred to as 'the beloved war' (*blessað stríðið*) in public parlance, because it improved the economic lot of the great majority of Icelanders.[11] At the beginning of the war, Iceland had suffered for years from a serious economic recession, which cast doubts on its viability as a sovereign state. The economic slump had started as the Great Depression spread to Iceland in the early 1930s, and was prolonged through the closing of its most important export market in Spain in the latter half of the decade. Iceland therefore lagged behind its neighbours in the late 1930s when Europe began to recover from the Depression. The situation changed swiftly after the spring of 1940, and in 1945 Iceland had surpassed Denmark, Norway and Finland in per capita GNP.[12] The rapid economic growth was directly related to the war. Most importantly, the 25,000 British soldiers stationed in Iceland in 1941[13] and the 50,000 mostly American soldiers in 1943[14] needed a range of services, while the foreign military was responsible for various construction projects providing employment for Icelandic workers. With a total population of just over 120,000 in 1940, Iceland was barely able to supply the workers needed by the foreign military forces, making chronic unemployment in Iceland disappear in one sweep. Anyone who wanted to work could find work with relative ease.[15] Another reason for the economic boom was the favourable market for Iceland's most important export products, cod in particular. Although access to important countries for Icelandic exports, such as Germany and Poland, had closed down at the beginning of the war, the lucrative British market more than compensated for the loss.[16] The British needed Icelandic fish and were willing to pay for it, and the Icelandic producers were more than happy to meet the demand.

The cultural impact of the war was felt with great anxiety by many leading members of Icelandic society. To them, the invasion of foreign ideas, language and lifestyles was a dangerous threat to Iceland's national identity and the country's moral order. The fear of foreign 'pollution' was especially acute when it came to what the male-dominated political class regarded as the more 'vulnerable' part of the nation, that is, the women and the young – and young women in particular. 'Hundreds of women have had too intimate contacts with the British occupation troops', declared a headline in the daily *Tíminn* one day in late August 1941. The occasion was the publication of an official report on the moral conduct of Icelandic women and their dealings with the British soldiers in Reykjavík. The situation was deadly serious, the report concluded, as there was a real danger that 'a large class of prostitutes will be formed here, who will abandon our civilised life.' The report did not advocate stringent restrictions on people's conduct, but recommended that every Icelander should be encouraged to do her or his duty. It was imperative to form a public opinion in Iceland which 'demanded both the protection of Icelandic nationality, Icelandic culture and Icelandic language, and that Iceland will continue to be an independent civilised nation. The future of the Icelandic nation depends on one thing only: that the country's youth do not forget their civic duty to their blood and soil [*blóð sitt og móðurmold*].'[17]

Looking at the Second World War from a distance, it is safe to conclude that Iceland was extremely fortunate during the years of carnage and destruction in Europe and beyond.[18] The British occupation and, from the summer of 1941, the American defence of Iceland were exceptionally benign when compared to the fate of most other small states in Europe under foreign military rule. The only interest the British and American authorities had in Iceland was to exploit the country's strategic location, and they rarely interfered in Icelandic domestic politics, doing their utmost not to antagonise the Icelandic politicians or the population at large. Moreover, at the end of the war, Iceland was economically more prosperous than it had ever been, and few seemed to doubt that it had the economic capacity to operate as a fully independent republic. But the war challenged many sacred political and cultural ideals in Iceland. Full independence had been the final aim of Icelandic politics for decades, or at least since beginning of the twentieth century. By the end of the war, Iceland had reached this utopian goal – its own *tausendjähriges Reich* – but it had happened through foreign invasion and occupation rather than through Icelandic actions. Moreover, Icelanders had an almost childlike belief in their cultural heritage, which they often hailed as one of the mainsprings of European civilisation. This is why language played such a central role in the construction of Icelandic nationalist identity and in the arguments of Icelandic nationalists during the early twentieth century. Most Icelanders fervently believed that they spoke the language of the Sagas more or less 'uncorrupted', regarding themselves the true heirs of a Nordic heritage. This linguistic 'purity' had been achieved through the relative isolation of the mid North Atlantic, which was aided by the fairly limited interest of the Danish authorities in 'civilising' the peasant tribe inhabiting their distant province. The war broke this splendid isolation, when the thousands of soldiers stationed in Iceland challenged the alleged purity of both Icelandic blood and culture. Thus, while the British and American armies kept the Germans at bay, their invasion undermined what Icelanders held most dear – and the defenders of the Icelandic moral order could do little more than pledge their allegiance to the Icelandic *Blut und Boden*.

The Second World War in Icelandic Historiography

The community of Icelandic historians is relatively small, as one would expect in a country which currently has just over 300,000 inhabitants. Trends in historical research often emerge and develop in a rather haphazard manner, reflecting the choices and interests of a very few individuals. In the case of the history of the Second World War, one historian, Þór Whitehead, professor of history at the University of Iceland, has dominated the scene for the last three decades. After defending his unpublished doctoral thesis at Oxford in 1978,[19] Whitehead launched the book series *Ísland í seinni heimsstyrjöld* ('Iceland in the Second World War'), which when completed will cover the whole war period. The books deal with, to quote the author, 'Iceland's relations with the military powers and Iceland's strategic importance during the World War 1939–45,'[20] surveying both the origins of the Second World War and Iceland's history during the war years. So far, Whitehead has completed four volumes in the series, covering mostly in a chronological order the period from the late 1930s to the beginning of the British occupation in the spring and summer of 1940: *Ófriður í aðsigi* ('A war approaching'), *Stríð fyrir ströndum* ('The war beyond the coast'), *Milli vonar og ótta* ('Between hope and fear'), and *Bretarnir koma* ('The British arrive').[21] All four volumes are based on meticulous research in Icelandic, German, British, and American archives and are both extremely detailed and very accessible to the general public. In fact, Whitehead purposely writes for the informed non-specialist, which makes his style both engaged and engaging. His books appeal to a fairly broad audience and have sold exceedingly well. He has clearly demonstrated that there is no lack of interest in the history of the Second World War among the general reading public in Iceland, although professional historians have not paid great attention to the subject.

In the introduction to the first volume of the series, Whitehead explains his general historiographical approach in the following manner:

> I am not one of those historians who believe that they can stand above the opinions of their own time, and deal with their subject from some undefined 'neutral' point of view. I adhere to certain principles, which it would be dishonest for me to hide. My goal is not to be 'neutral', but to search for the truth and explain it.[22]

It is far from obvious what Whitehead means by this methodological declaration, but it has to be read in the context of his general political outlook. He has never concealed his support of the Independence Party and its conservative, pro-American policies, which has positioned him decisively in the Icelandic political landscape. Moreover, he has not shied away from controversy when his interpretations of the past have been challenged. This has led to heated polemics on the history of the Communist movement in Iceland, especially on the role of Comintern in the formation of the Socialist Unity Party in 1937–1938.[23] But so far, his conclusions on the history of the Second World War have not been seriously contested and his version of the truth has therefore been generally accepted by his political adversaries as well as his allies.[24]

Such consensus is, of course, partly testimony to the quality of Whitehead's scholarship.[25] But it also reflects the fact that Icelandic wartime politics have never been a source of much controversy – except, perhaps, during the first years of the war itself. In an article Whitehead wrote in 1979, commemorating the thirtieth anniversary of the foundation of the NATO, he argues that the Icelandic defence policy, from the time Iceland became a sovereign state in 1918 and through the Cold War, was marked by an uneasy balancing act between pragmatism and nationalism.[26] In the years between the two world wars, the idea of neutrality was motivated by the desire to keep Iceland free from foreign interference, or to preserve what was seen as the nation's sacred right to sovereignty. This principle was, however, always tempered by the realisation of the country's inability to defend itself from foreign aggression. During the inter-war years, Whitehead argues, the Icelandic authorities had full faith in Britain's ability to police North Atlantic waters, accepting the fact that the country was situated in the British sphere of influence. At the same time, the Icelanders refused to make any formal commitment to the British cause in the war and resented every pressure to submit to British control over Icelandic policies. Neutrality, in their eyes, meant that Iceland should have the right to deal freely with whomever it desired, including Germany and its allies, while the country continued to enjoy de facto protection by the British fleet. Iceland was a very reluctant ally, as the American political scientist Donald E. Nuechterlein has it.[27] It was only willing to take sides in international disputes when it was forced to, and even then, did so very grudgingly.

The dominating policy during the Second World War, which we could label as the nationalist-pragmatist approach, enjoyed widespread contemporary support in Iceland. This has undoubtedly contributed to the universal acceptance of Whitehead's analysis. Throughout the war years, the Icelandic authorities pledged their belief in Iceland's absolute neutrality, which had only been temporarily suspended in 1940 when circumstances were overpowering. As much was made clear in 1945 when Iceland refused to declare war on the Axis powers, which was required if it was to become a founding member of the United Nations.[28] Although eager to join the UN, the Icelandic government valued Iceland's neutrality more highly than the desire of entering the post-war world as a formal member of the group of Allied nations. With this decision, the government refused to take any responsibility for the war, although it was clear that it had transformed Iceland's place in the world. This tension between active participation in the international arena and the desire to keep the world at bay characterised Icelandic foreign policy during the next decades, splitting Icelandic society into two hostile camps for much of the Cold War.

The political friction of the Cold War, which revolved mostly around the stationing of American soldiers in Iceland and around Iceland's NATO membership, did not affect people's attitudes to the Second World War and Iceland's position in it. Everyone agreed that Iceland's participation in the war was not of its own volition, and no Icelandic politician or political movement could therefore be blamed for dragging the country into the conflict. Moreover, as the Allies were victorious in the war, few have ever doubted the moral legitimacy of their cause. Finally, Iceland's situation in the war has freed it from suggestions of anti-Semitism or participation in the Holocaust, although it has been pointed out that the Icelandic authorities were far from welcoming toward Jewish refugees who sought asylum in the years leading up to the conflict – in part because they wanted to protect the 'purity' of the Icelandic 'race'.[29] For this reason, the active and extensive cooperation with the Allied military forces in Iceland, or, to use Johan Östling's term, the Icelandic version of 'small-state realism', has never carried with it the same moral stigma as similar activities in countries under German occupation or influence in Europe. The 'cooperation' with the British and Americans forces was thus not 'collaboration' or a betrayal of the Icelandic nation, but has rather been interpreted as necessary and justified, even just. This is why the interest in, or moral incentive of, rewriting the history of Iceland's participation in the Second World War, or to present an alternative narrative to the nationalist-pragmatist thesis, has been limited at best.

The most notable exception to this lack of moral concern relates to people's attitudes toward relationships between Icelandic women and the foreign soldiers stationed in Iceland, known as 'the situation' (*ástandið*) at the time. As mentioned before, the alleged 'pollution' of Icelandic blood through sexual relationships between native women and foreign men was fiercely resisted, especially during the early stages of the war. In contemporary political discourses, Icelandic women were regarded as a 'biological resource',[30] which had to be protected – even from the protectors.[31] Attitudes of this kind were always coloured by male anxiety, as Icelandic men feared competition from the huge number of young male foreigners stationed in their midst. The war also opened up new employment opportunities for Icelandic women, challenging the traditional patriarchal family and power structures. To limit communication between Icelandic women and the foreigners, Icelandic officials suggested that the soldiers should not be allowed to enter Icelandic homes, and the widespread custom of hiring women to wash the soldiers' laundry was to be ended.[32] The most effective tool in discouraging the undesired sexual relations with foreign soldiers was, however, the stigmatisation of the women who were suspected of having intimate relations with the British or American soldiers. They could be branded as morally suspect, if not as prostitutes. This stigma was maintained in post-war novels and other literary works, where women who had had a relationship with the foreign soldiers were often described as shallow and unenlightened, unaware of Icelandic cultural traditions and history.[33] According to this view, their choices of partner signified a lack of patriotism and moral integrity, and had to be condemned. Interestingly, such attitudes were much less pronounced in works written by women authors than they were in those written by their male colleagues, reflecting the gendered outlook on this sensitive issue. To many women, the presence of a large number of foreign soldiers in the country presented opportunities they had never had before, and they saw no reason not to pursue them. The nationalist discourse on 'the situation', at least if we accept the feminist interpretation, was therefore simply a veiled attempt to preserve traditional male authority in Icelandic society. The nation was not only to remain Icelandic, but it was also to be dominated by Icelandic men.[34]

The 'Bootstrap Theory'

The place of the Second World War in Icelandic historiography was already set during its latter stages. This can be seen from the celebrations around the foundation of the Icelandic republic, which were launched on 17 June 1944. The most important event took place at the historical site of Þingvellir, where the newly elected president of Iceland, Sveinn Björnsson, signed the new republican constitution into law. Both the day and the location of this ceremony were carefully chosen for symbolic reasons: 17 June was the birthday of the Icelandic national hero, the nineteenth-century philologist Jón Sigurðsson, while Þingvellir (literally the Assembly or Parliamentary Plains) was the place where members of the Icelandic elite had gathered every summer from the tenth century until the end of the 1700s to attend an assembly called Alþingi. By linking the founding of the republic with both the name of the unquestioned instigator of the Icelandic nationalist movement and with the place 'where the heart of the [Icelandic] nation beats,' to quote a former prime minister of Iceland,[35] the foundation of the republic was firmly anchored in the history of the Icelandic nation. The message to the world was that this was an *Icelandic* event, the result of *Icelandic* actions, and a fulfilment of an *Icelandic* dream.[36]

In spite of the nationalist tenor of the event, it was difficult to conceal its international context. The ceremony at Þingvellir occurred in the shadow of the Second World War and it was marked by this fact in a number of ways. Less than two weeks earlier, the Allied forces had landed on the beaches of Normandy, and while the Icelandic nation celebrated its independence, the Americans, the British and their allies were still consolidating their position in northern France. Moreover, when the ties with Denmark were finally severed and King Christian X was officially deposed as the king of Iceland, Denmark was still under German occupation and its leaders were thus unable to respond effectively to Iceland's demands and actions. Finally, when President Sveinn Björnsson signed the new constitution at Þingvellir, there were thousands of American and British soldiers stationed in Iceland, and the Icelandic authorities therefore needed the consent of the Allied authorities before they could pursue their plans to seek full independence from Denmark.[37] Although the war was certainly not the only reason for the secession from Denmark, as the Act of Union between Iceland and Denmark had stipulated that either party could abrogate it unilaterally after 1943,[38] the war had, for all practical purposes, made the foundation of the republic inevitable.

Despite its obvious significance, it seems that the Icelandic authorities had little interest in factoring the Second World War into the history of the republic. An official exhibition, commemorating the foundation of the new regime by surveying the history of Iceland from its beginnings to the establishment of the republic, is a perfect example of such historiographic ambivalence. The exhibition opened on 20 June 1944, with President Björnsson, the Icelandic government, members of parliament and foreign ambassadors in attendance.[39] According to the exhibition catalogue, the organisers sought to provide 'glimpses from the Icelandic cultural struggle and its struggle for freedom from the beginning of Icelandic history to the present day', while the exhibition was also 'to evoke memories of certain occurrences and events' in the story of the Icelandic nation.[40] In this spirit, the exhibition celebrated what its organisers regarded as the most memorable phases, developments and occurrences in the history of the nation and its most important accomplishments, ranging from the settlement of Iceland in the ninth and tenth centuries to the foundation of Alþingi in the early tenth century, the literary achievements of the saga period, the explorations and voyages in the Middle Ages, the struggle for independence in the nineteenth century and the economic modernisation of the early twentieth century. It also presented some of the less glorious historical chapters, lamenting 'the national decline and humiliation' under Norwegian and Danish rule. The Second World War was, however, conspicuously absent from this historical narrative. The only time it was referred to, as far as can be seen from existing descriptions of the exhibition, was in connection with an anecdote describing the courage and stoicism of an Icelandic fisherman when faced with the dangers of sailing on the high seas during the war. His response to a German attack was compared with the deeds of medieval Viking explorers and interpreted as an undisputable sign of the unbroken link between modern Icelandic seafarers and their ancestors in the past.[41] The implication was that even if the political and economic conditions of the nation had changed dramatically over eleven hundred years of Icelandic history, the 'national character' had remained essentially unaltered.

The absence of the Second World War from the historical exhibition was hardly a coincidence, as its declared intention was to highlight the importance of self-determination for the cultural and economic wellbeing of the nation. The history of Iceland was, to quote the exhibition catalogue, 'an exceptionally clear example of the fact that the flower of culture cannot grow but in the soil of freedom',[42] and this message had to be communicated to all Icelanders. Another prominent theme in the exhibition was the idea that the economic development of the Icelandic nation was organically related to its political sovereignty. In the seven decades that had passed from 1874, when the Icelandic parliament received limited legislative power, the country had moved from practically medieval conditions into modernity, the author of the catalogue maintained.[43] This was interpreted as irrefutable proof of the benefits of political freedom. The last room of the exhibition, titled 'Self-determination', was devoted to the process of modernisation, demonstrating how 'the great and daring progress' in Iceland had been directly related to 'the increasing autonomy of the nation'. For this reason, 'the years 1874, 1903, 1918 and 1944[44] were generally selected as examples', the catalogue stated, as they were regarded as the clearest markers of the nation's rush toward both modernity and full independence.[45] To illustrate this point further, the organisers had collected a variety of demographic and economic statistics and photographs of the symbols of Icelandic modernity, portraying electrical power plants, trawlers, modern school buildings, etc. These signs of Icelandic modernisation were exhibited under a motto, taken from a nineteenth-century patriotic poem: 'The world will sentence you to slavery, unless you will be liberated through your own efforts.'[46]

This historical approach was a variation on a traditional theme in Icelandic national historiography, where it has been assumed that the nation had literally pulled itself up from poverty by its own bootstraps, or propelled itself, solely through its own effort, from medieval conditions into the modern world. The underlying idea was, as was stated in the exhibition catalogue, that a 'nation which had accomplished all this and not troubled other nations, deserves to be free and to lead its life in peace.'[47] According to this theory, there was a double causal link between national liberty and progress: national liberty was a precondition for people's material and cultural advancement, while the apparent cultural and economic progress of the nation during the first half of the twentieth century legitimised its freedom. The nationalist vision was rooted in the hegemonic interpretation of Icelandic history, which served as a key to interpreting the nation's past and as an intellectual map for its future. This interpretation, or historical plot, appeared in fully developed form at the beginning of the twentieth century in the works of the historian Jón Jónsson, who was appointed professor of history at the University of Iceland at its foundation in 1911. In his book *Íslenzkt þjóðerni* ('Icelandic Nationality'), published in 1903, he divided the history of Iceland into five periods, each with its specific character and particular disposition toward the outside world. First was the period of *self-determination*, which lasted until the country became part of the Norwegian monarchy in the late thirteenth century. This was a time of exceptional prosperity and cultural vitality in Iceland, Jónsson alleged, when Icelandic culture was on a par with Greek culture at its peak during the classical period. Second was the period of *decline*, spanning from the late thirteenth century to the Reformation (in the mid sixteenth century). During this period the nation resisted negative influences from abroad, seeking to maintain its independence against Norwegian, and later Danish, rule. Third was the period of *humiliation*, which lasted from the mid sixteenth century to the middle of the 1700s. According to Jónsson, this was a time of growing foreign control in Iceland, which resulted in the ever-increasing poverty and lethargy of the Icelandic population. The fourth period was the Icelandic *renaissance*, when patriotic intellectuals roused the nation from its protracted slumber by introducing ideas of the Enlightenment and Romantic nationalism to common Icelanders. Following cultural regeneration in the early nineteenth century, demands for national self-determination grew louder, followed by the first steps toward political autonomy. Finally, Jónsson proposed that Iceland was entering its fifth period at the time when his book was written. This was the age of *progress*, which commenced with the Icelandic home-rule government in 1904. In the eyes of the nationalists, it was the beginning of a new golden era, or a return to self-determination after seven centuries of foreign rule. This would surely, they claimed, bring with it rapid economic modernisation, cultural regeneration, and ever-growing prosperity to the nation.[48] 'What the nation was in the past', wrote Jónsson, 'we can hope it can become again.'[49] The paradise lost would only be reclaimed, though, after the nation had regained its freedom.

The Second World War contradicted this line of argument in a fundamental manner. During the war years, as has been pointed out, Iceland experienced unprecedented material prosperity, when the country was under tighter and more effective foreign control than ever before in its history. To reconcile this discrepancy between what can be called a historical myth (emphasising the organic link between 'freedom' and 'progress') and reality (the rapid economic growth under foreign rule), Icelandic commentators tended to regard the war years as a digression from the 'natural' course of Icelandic history, or simply as an anomaly of limited consequence for the general narrative of the nation. This attitude can be seen in the words of Gunnar Thoroddsen, professor of law at the University of Iceland and a rising star of the Independence Party, which he expressed in a public address on the 'sovereign day', 1 December 1945. 'Our origins and character, nationality and culture, oblige us to seek unfettered self-determination', he stated, rejecting out of hand all requests from the US to be allowed to prolong their military presence in Iceland after the war. 'Our experience and history guide us, without any reservation, on the same track. Every restriction on our national freedom hampers the nation's development and decreases its prosperity; every step toward freedom has moved the nation toward more maturity and improved its conditions.'[50] With the war over, it was time to return to the national politics of the past, to defend the unconditional sovereignty of the nation.

Toward New Historical Paradigms?

'Nationalism is partly a matter of narrative construction, the production (and reproduction and revision) of narratives locating the nation's place and history', claims the American sociologist Craig Calhoun in a recent appraisal of modern nationalism. In other words, 'nations move through historical time as persons move through biographical time; each may figure in stories like characters in a novel.'[51] According to this view, national histories are instrumental in the construction and preservation of all nations and national identities. One may argue, however, that history has played a larger role in Icelandic nationalism than in many other nations'. The reason lies in the marked discrepancy between Iceland's situation at the beginning of its development toward sovereign statehood and the Icelanders' desire for national self-determination. During the nineteenth and early twentieth centuries, most foreign commentators agreed that it was sheer 'madness for a population of 70,000 to request an independent statehood', to quote a letter from the eminent Danish intellectual Georg Brandes to the Icelandic poet and pastor Matthías Jochumsson in 1907. 'You have no trade, no industry, no army, no fleet, you are altogether as numerous as a small, fifth-rate town in England and Germany; the only thing you have is a famous past ...'[52] Icelandic interpretations of the country's situation were diametrically different, because Icelandic observers generally regarded what Brandes called Iceland's 'famous past' as a clear argument for national independence. In their reading of Icelandic history, the alleged glory of the medieval 'Golden Age', the apparent decline under Norwegian and Danish rule, and the rapid modernisation in the late nineteenth and early twentieth centuries were all indisputable arguments for the benefits of sovereignty and indications of the adverse effects of foreign rule. Progress was therefore not a precondition for national sovereignty, but sovereignty was rather a necessary precondition for any nation to prosper.

This was the gist of the story which the organisers of the historical exhibition in Reykjavík presented to the citizens of the newly-established Republic of Iceland during the summer of 1944, and it has been the guiding principle of the official Icelandic historical discourse ever since. 'Freedom was the source of energy which had been lacking for so long', wrote Prime Minister Davíð Oddsson in January 2004 in reference to the foundation of Icelandic home rule one century earlier. 'Faint hopes had certainly resided with the nation, and it had its dreams and desires, but the right to take the initiative rested on the wrong shoulders until Iceland was awarded home-rule government.'[53]

Although one might expect that the Second World War was a central period in the biography of the Icelandic nation, to paraphrase Craig Calhoun, it has received fairly limited attention in its historiography. Iceland took the final steps toward independence during the war, and its economy and place in international politics were transformed during the years of conflict. These years can therefore be seen as a formative period in the life of the modern Icelandic nation. It appears, however, that the history of the war years has challenged the general storyline of the Icelandic national narrative.

This particular history has been relegated to a historiographical limbo: everyone agrees that the Second World War was an important period for Iceland, but in many ways it has been treated as 'foreign history' rather than as an integral part of Icelandic history.

In recent years, Icelandic academics have revised or deconstructed many of the national – or nationalist – myths of the Icelandic grand narrative, but the Second World War does not loom large in that revision.[54] In part, this was a direct consequence of what has been argued above; that is, the traditional national narrative sets the revisionists' agenda. But, in part this was also caused by the lack of research on the history of the war in Iceland. This will certainly change when Þór Whitehead's much-anticipated survey of the war years in Iceland is completed, as it will provide a firm factual basis for other historians to work with. If this will lead to a new historical paradigm in Iceland remains to be seen, but it will certainly make it possible.

Notes

1 Valur Ingimundarson, 'Saga utanríkismála á 20. öld', *Saga*, 38, 2000, 207–227; the survey of the historiography of the Second World War is at 210–211.

2 See, for example, Tómas Þór Tómasson, *Heimsstyrjaldarárin á Íslandi 1939–1945*, 2 vols. (Reykjavík, 1983–1984), and Helgi Skúli Kjartansson, *Ísland á 20. öld* (Reykjavík, 2002), 213–269.

3 See Guðmundur. Hálfdanarson, 'Severing the Ties – Iceland's Journey from a Union with Denmark to a Nation-State', *Scandinavian Journal of History*, 31, 2006:3/4, 237–254.

4 *Alþingistíðindi 1925* D (Reykjavík, 1925), 743–744.

5 Ólafur Thors, 'Áramót', *Morgunblaðið*, 31 December 1939, 3.

6 See Þór Whitehead, *Bretarnir koma* (Reykjavík, 1999).

7 'Ávarp forsætisráðherra til þjóðarinnar í gærkvöldi', *Alþýðublaðið*, 11 May 1940, 3, and 'Forsætisráðherra skýrir þjóðinni frá atburðunum', *Tíminn*, 11 May 1940, 201 and 204.

8 See for example 'Ísland í höndum nasista hefði þýtt ósigur Bretlands', *Lesbók Morgunblaðsins*, 15 September 1974:4–5; Þór Whitehead, *Ófriður í aðsigi* (Reykjavík, 1980), 286–303, and Whitehead 1999, 56–60.

9 'Vér mótmælum allir', *Þjóðviljinn*, 11 May 1940, 2.

10 'Íslendingar! Allir eitt gegn fasismanum', *Þjóðviljinn*, 13 May 1942, 3–4; see also Valur Ingimundarson, *Ísland í eldlínu kalda stríðsins. Samskipti Íslands og Bandaríkjanna 1945–1960* (Reykjavík, 1996), 23–24.

11 This expression can be traced back to the First World War, but is now com-

monly used to signify the Second World War in Iceland; see 'Reykjavíkurbrjef', *Morgunblaðið*, 19 July 1942, 5; Bjarni Guðmarsson, *Saga Keflavíkur*, vol. III. *1920–1949* (Reykjanesbær, 1999), 361, and Jón Hjaltason, *Hernámsárin á Akureyri og Eyjafirði* (Akureyri, 1991), 21.

12 Guðmundur Jónsson, *Hagvöxtur og iðnvæðing: Þróun landsframleiðslu á Íslandi 1870–1945* (Reykjavík, 1999), 174–179, 387.

13 Donald F. Bittner, *The Lion and the White Falcon: Britain and Iceland in the World War II Era* (Hamden, CT, 1983), 61.

14 Pétur J. Thorsteinsson, *Utanríkisþjónusta Íslands og utanríkismál: Sögulegt yfirlit*, (Reykjavík, 1992), 216–217.

15 See Magnús S. Magnússon & Guðmundur Jónsson (eds.), *Hagskinna: Icelandic Historical Statistics* (Reykjavík, 1997), 91 and 245.

16 See Tómas Þór Tómasson, *Heimsstyrjaldarárin á Íslandi 1939–1945*, vol. II (Reykjavík, 1984), 146–165.

17 'Hundruð kvenna í Reykjavík hafa of náin afskipti af setuliðinu', *Tíminn*, 29 August 1941, 346 and 348; see also 'Skuggalegar myndir af siðferði reykvískra kvenna', *Morgunblaðið*, 28 August 1941. The last words of the report should not, in themselves, be understood as a reference to Nazi ideology, but rather as a variation on a common theme in Icelandic nationalist discourses, where the people (the nation), the land and the Icelandic culture (the language) are seen as one organic whole. The words do, however, indicate how pervasive some of the underlying ideas of National Socialism were in European politics during the first half of the twentieth century.

18 It is estimated that 225 Icelanders lost their lives because of the war. Most of them perished at sea after German attacks on Icelandic ships; see Gunnar M. Magnúss, *Virkið í norðri: Sæfarendur*, vol. III (Reykjavík, 1950), and Tómasson 1984, 159–162.

19 Þór Whitehead, 'Iceland in the Second World War, 1939–1946', Ph.D. diss., Oxford University, 1978.

20 Whitehead 1980, 8.

21 Þór Whitehead, *Ófriður í aðsigi* (Reykjavík, 1980), *Stríð fyrir ströndum* (Reykjavík, 1985), *Milli vonar og ótta* (Reykjavík, 1995), and *Bretarnir koma* (Reykjavík, 1999). He has also published one book of photographs from the war years in Iceland, *Ísland í hers höndum* (Reykjavík, 2002) and another on the attempts of the German authorities to gain influence in Iceland before the war – *Íslandsævintýri Himmlers 1935–1937* (Reykjavík, 1988; 2nd edn Reykjavík, 1998).

22 Whitehead 1980, 9.

23 Jón Ólafsson, 'Komintern gegn klofningi: Viðbrögð Alþjóðasambands kommúnista við stofnun Sósíalistaflokksins', *Saga*, 45, 2007:1, 93–111; Þór Whitehead, 'Eftir skilyrðum Kominterns. Stofnun Sameingarflokks alþýðu – Sósíalistaflokksins 1937–1938', *Saga*, 46, 2008:2, 17–55; Jón Ólafsson, 'Rauveruleiki fortíðar og eitt minnisblað', *Saga*, 47, 2009:1, 149–161; Þór Whitehead, 'Eitt minnisblað og óraunveruleiki fortíðar: Svar til Jóns Ólafssonar', *Saga*, 47, 2009:2, 175–184; Jón Ólafsson, 'Nokkur orð um ályktanir og túlkun heimilda', *Saga*, 48, 2010:1, 165–172.

24 See, for example Árni Bergmann, 'Klippt og skorið', *Þjóðviljinn*, 13 December 1985, 4, and Björn Bjarnason, 'Stríðið nálgast Ísland', *Morgunblaðið*, 11 December 1985, 18–19.

25 The praise is not universal, though; see Sigurður Líndal, 'Ísland og aðdragandi heimsstyrjaldar 1939–45', *Skírnir*, 155, 1981, 171–203.

26 Þór Whitehead, 'Raunsæi *og* þjóðernisstefna: Aðdragandinn að inngöngu Íslands í NATO', *Morgunblaðið II*, 4 April 1979, 47–50; see also Whitehead 1980, 47–49.

27 Donald E. Nuechterlein, *Iceland: A Reluctant Ally* (Ithaca, NY, 1961).

28 Valur Ingimundarson, *Í eldlínu kalda stríðsins: Samskipti Íslands og Bandaríkjanna 1945–1960* (Reykjavík, 1996), 36–38; Þór Whitehead, 'Hlutleysi Íslands á hverfanda hveli 1918–1945', *Saga*, 44, 2006:1, 46–61.

29 Whitehead 1980, 85–91; Vilhjálmur Örn Vilhjálmsson, *Medaljens bagside: Jødiske flygtiningeskæbner i Danmark 1933–1945* (Copenhagen, 2005), 8–13.

30 See Unnur B. Karlsdóttir, *Mannkynbætur: Hugmyndir um bætta kynstofna hérlendis og erlendis á 19. og 20. öld* (Reykjavík, 1998), 110–111.

31 Gunnar M. Magnúss, *Virkið í norðri: Þríbýlisárin*, vol. II (Reykjavík, 1947), 619–672.

32 See the letter of the Icelandic Surgeon General from 1941 in Magnúss 1947, 652–653.

33 Inga Dóra Björnsdóttir, 'Íslenskar konur og erlendir hermenn í augum fimm íslenskra skálda', in *Íslenskar kvennarannsóknir 29. ágúst–1. sept. 1985* (Reykjavík, 1985), 206–214.

34 See Björnsdóttir 1985 and I.D. Björnsdóttir, 'Island: Uheldige kvinner i et heldig land', in: D. Ellingsen, A. Warring & I.D. Björnsdóttir (eds.), *Kvinner, krig og kjærlighet* (Oslo, 1995), 149–196; Bára Baldursdóttir, '"Þær myndu fegnar skipta um þjóðerni". Ríkisafskipti af samböndum unglingsstúlkna og setuliðsmanna', in: A. Agnarsdóttir, E.H. Halldórsdóttir, H. Gísladóttir, I.H. Hákonardóttir, S. Matthíasdóttir & S.K. Þorgrímsdóttir (eds.), *Kvennaslóðir: Rit til heiðurs Sigríði Th. Erlendsdóttur sagnfræðingi* (Reykjavík, 2001), 302–317; Herdís Helgadóttir, *Úr fjötrum: Íslenskar konur og erlendur her* (Reykjavík, 2001).

35 Davíð Oddsson, 'Hátíðisdagur á helgum degi', in: Ingólfur Margeirsson (ed.), *Þjóð á Þingvöllum* (Reykjavík, 1994), 7.

36 See Guðmundur Hálfdanarson, 'Þingvellir: An Icelandic "Lieu de Mémoire"', *History and Memory*, 12, 2000:1, 4–29.

37 Björn Þórðarson, *Alþingi og frelsisbaráttan 1874–1944* (Reykjavík, 1951), 510–513; Þór Whitehead, 'Stórveldin og lýðveldið 1941–1944', *Skírnir*, 147, 1973, 202–241; and Sólrún B. Jensdóttir Hardarson, 'The "Republic of Iceland" 1940–44: Anglo-American Attitudes and Influences', *Journal of Contemporary History*, 9, 1974:4, 27–56.

38 'Dansk-íslensk sambandslög', *Stjórnartíðindi fyrir Ísland* A (Reykjavík, 1918), 75–79. According to the Act of Union, the Icelandic and Danish governments were to start negotiations on its renewal in 1940, and only if they broke down could either party abrogate the agreement between the two nations unilaterally. As these negotiations never took place, because of the war, Iceland's actions

in 1944 were technically a breech of the contract from 1918.

39 See, for example, 'Söguleg sýning úr frelsis- og menningarbaráttu Íslendinga', *Alþýðublaðið*, 21 June 1944, 2, and 'Frelsi og menning: Hin sögulega sýning í Menntaskólanum', *Morgunblaðið*, 21 June 1944, 2.

40 *Frelsi og menning: Sýning úr frelsis- og menningarbaráttu Íslendinga í Menntaskólanum í Reykjavík í júní 1944* (Reykjavík, 1944), 5.

41 Einar Olgeirsson, 'Sögusýningin', in: *Lýðveldishátíðin 1944* (Reykjavík, 1945), 399.

42 *Frelsi og menning*, 11. The author is not mentioned, but according to one member of the organising committee, it was written by Professor Einar Ólafur Sveinsson at the University of Iceland; Einar Olgeirsson, 1945, 383.

43 See *Frelsi og menning*, 42.

44 These years were seen as the most important stepping stones on Iceland's route to independence: in 1874, Iceland received its first constitution, endowing the Icelandic parliament, Alþingi, with limited legislative authority in Icelandic domestic affairs; in 1903, the king signed the Icelandic home-rule constitution; in 1918 Iceland became a sovereign state in a union with Denmark; and in 1944, the republic was founded.

45 Olgeirsson, 1945, 423–426.

46 Olgeirsson, 1945, 422–426.

47 *Frelsi og menning*, 42.

48 Jón Jónsson, *Íslenzkt þjóðerni* (Reykjavík, 1903), 237–257 and passim.

49 Jónsson 1903, 256.

50 Gunnar Thoroddsen, 'Fullveldið og herstöðvar', *Morgunblaðið*, 2 December 1945, 2.

51 Craig Calhoun, *Nations Matter: Culture, History, and the Cosmopolitan Dream* (London, 2007), 45.

52 In Francis Bull & John Landquist (eds.), *Georg og Edv. Brandes: Brevveksling med nordiske Forfattere og Videnskabsmænd*, vol. III (Copenhagen, 1940), 412–414.

53 D. Oddsson, 'Vandinn við að varðveita og efla frelsið flóknari en nokkru sinni fyrr', *Morgunblaðið*, 2 January 2004, 20–21.

54 See, for example Hilma Gunnarsdóttir, 'Íslenska söguendurskoðunin: Aðferðir og hugmyndir í sagnfræði á áttunda og níunda áratug tuttugustu aldar', in: H. Gunnarsdóttir, J.Þ. Pétursson & S.G. Magnússon (eds.), *Frá endurskoðun til upplausnar* (Reykjavík, 2006), 23–110; Guðmundur Hálfdanarson, 'Collective Memory, History, and National Identity', in: Á. Eysteinsson (ed.), *The Cultural Construction of Places* (Reykjavík, 2006), 83–100.

CHAPTER 5

The Solidity of a National Narrative

The German Occupation in Norwegian History Culture

Synne Corell

In the Norwegian public sphere, the years of German occupation between 1940 and 1945 are commonly referred to as *krigen*, the War. Throughout the post-war era, there have been repeated predictions that the attention paid to these five years would decrease. Yet, books and feature newspaper continue to be published, films are made, and issues related to this period are debated in different public arenas. Even if the years of German occupation have been ascribed special significance ever since the events unfolded, it is reasonable to ask if the persistent interest represents continuity, or if it is more productive to imagine 'the War' as holding varying political, cultural and moral values for different agents and at different points in time. The focal point in this chapter is to examine if certain events connected to the end of the Cold War should be understood to have contributed to a new understanding in Norway of the years of German occupation. I will therefore start by outlining some defining aspects of the history writing on the occupation up to the 1980s in order to take a closer look at three historical controversies in Norway – the first in the late 1980s and the other two in the 1990s – in an attempt to uncover potential changes in the way the occupation has been assessed.

The Main Dichotomy – *Nasjonal Samling* vs. 'Good Norwegians'

National histories can be read as narratives about a community of 'us' and 'our' enemies or opponents.[1] In the narratives of Norway during the Second World War, the role of the nation's 'other' has invariably been assigned to representatives of the German occupation regime and the Norwegian National Socialist party, *Nasjonal Samling* (NS). Led by Vidkun Quisling, the NS was declared the only legal political party in Norway in the autumn of 1940. With support from the German occupiers, Quisling was formally installed as 'Minister President' in 1942. The bulk of the history writing on the German occupation has been polarised: on the one hand the representatives of the German occupational forces, Quisling, and central politicians from the NS; on the other hand the King, the government in exile in the UK, and other agents within certain public or illegal arenas: the bureaucracy, the armed forces, the church, the organizations, and illegal groups.

The members of the NS, backed by the German occupants, have been perceived as constituting the opposite pole of the 'good Norwegians' of the Norwegian majority, symbolised primarily by King Haakon VII. In an article from 2009, the historian Ole Kristian Grimnes argues that 'the post-war national story about the years of occupation has been spun around this dichotomy. The history writing of the occupation obtained its foundational structure.'[2] Grimnes argues that this dichotomy can still be said to prevail, in the sense that subsequent history writing and memory culture has moderated the understanding of two poles instead of undoing the fundamental premises of this construction. In giving later history writing the role of either 'moderating' or 'undoing' the construction, Grimnes plays down the possibility that historians might be seen as having created, enforced or revived a polarised understanding of the war years.

I will argue that a nationally framed understanding has held, and in many ways still holds, a prominent position in Norwegian historiography and memory culture. By using the term 'nationally framed', I wish to highlight three tendencies that can be understood as both separate and interconnected in the narratives of Norway during the Second World War: the construction of a homogenous Norwegian community; the narratives as negotiations of national identity; and the nation-state as the prearranged entity of history writing and the given scene for debates on war memory. It thus describes an understanding of a polarised Norwegian community where the group in opposition to NS and the occupiers is portrayed as a majority where social, political, cultural and ethnic diversities are minimised or even ignored, thus constructing Norwegian wartime society as homogenous or monocultural. Many historical writings and debates on war memory can be read as 'nationally framed' in the sense that they negotiate national identity by distributing agency and ascertaining who were the heroes, perpetrators and victims, for example, through concepts of adaptation, collaboration and resistance. Finally, a nationally framed focus on the years of occupation potentially collides with the conceptualisation of the Second World War as a total war, an industrialised conflict on an immense scale, geographically and in terms of the aims and modes of fighting. The historian Odd-Bjørn Fure argues that certain aspects and perspectives have been left out of the historical studies of Norway during the war precisely because this research has been carried out within the perspective of the nation-state.[3] The fate of the Soviet, Yugoslav and Polish prisoners of war (POWs) brought to Norway by the Germans are an example of a topic which has an unstable position in the national framework.[4] A 'national framework' can in this context be understood both as the historians' potential mirroring of a certain disposition in the collective war memory and the result of the central place the nation-state has had in modern historiography.

Professional historians in Norway have not only had a decisive impact on the construction of the interpretations of the War, and their audience has not only included their professional colleagues but also the wider public. A great many texts have been published about Norway during the Second World War, and the numbers keep growing. The history of the occupation has been addressed not only by academic historians, but to a large degree by journalists and amateur historians.[5] Even if this ideally calls for an all-embracing intertextual approach to this historiographical field, such an approach is beyond the scope of this chapter.[6] As Sivert Langholm has observed, a characteristic feature of Norwegian post-war historical culture is the number of multi-volume history works financed by publishing houses and written by professional historians for a non-professional public.[7]

Since the 1950s, Norwegian and world-history has unfolded in five multi-volume histories ranging from nine to twenty volumes. Two multi-volume works and a one-volume work of reference have been published since 1945 about the Second World War and the occupation: the three-volume *Norges krig* ('Norway's war') came out in 1947–1950, while *Norge i krig* ('Norway at war'), published in 1984–1987, comprises fully eight volumes. The final publication is a one-volume work of reference, *Norsk krigsleksikon 1940–45* ('Norwegian war encyclopaedia 1940–45'), published in 1995.[8] The publication of such national histories demonstrates the importance attributed to the years of occupation, and I will refer to these works as representing the central interpretations of 'the War' in post-war Norway. With leading historians as editors and authors, the three series are the only comprehensive works written exclusively on this subject for a wider Norwegian audience in the post-war period.

Norges krig (1947–1950)

The first of these histories, *Norges krig*, points to some significant aspects of the interpretation of the war in early post-war Norway. Published in the immediate aftermath of the war, in 1947 to 1950, *Norges krig* is the first multi-volume work on the subject. The series was edited by Sverre Steen, a prominent Norwegian historian of the day, yet the majority of authors were not academic historians, but rather had been key figures during the war, and several of them also held central positions in the Norwegian post-war society. Also, as they represented different and sometimes overlapping war communities, they invested their prestige and political interests both in their handling of the war years and in the situation they found themselves in when they contributed to *Norges krig*. In some cases, the two perspectives – past and present – must have been inextricably linked.

The definition of 'resistance' as a broad national movement, *holdningskamp* or the struggle for attitudes or minds, is a significant feature of *Norges krig*. According to this line, the so-called good Norwegians resisted the NS regime, either spiritually or materially. 'Resistance' in *Norges krig* sometimes refers to a small and exclusive unit, at other times to the wider community and a broad national movement in the struggle against the occupiers and their supporters. This conceptualisation of 'resistance' has been a key facet of much later history writing. In its widest sense, 'resistance' blurs active and passive resistance and can therefore close the gap between a symbolic struggle for hearts and minds and active acts of sabotage.

Norges krig focuses to a great degree on the work done by the government in exile in London and other agents in certain public or illegal arenas. In this narrative, 'resistance' has just as much to do with responsibility and restraint as with action and military achievement. This representation mirrors the scepticism toward active, military resistance shared for a long time by the government in exile and their officially approved resistance movements, *Milorg* and *Hjemmefronten*. *Milorg* was a military organisation recognised by the government in exile in 1941 as part of the Norwegian armed forces, while *Hjemmefronten* – 'the Home Front' – refers both to the idealised pole of 'good Norwegians', 'resistance' as mental reservation, and the organised resistance movement. The name *Hjemmefrontens ledelse* (HL, the leadership of Home Front) was adopted in the spring of 1944 for cooperation between the civilian resistance groupings *Kretsen* (the Circle) and *Koordinasjonskomiteen* (the Coordinating Committee). As of 1943, the civilian leadership cooperated with *Milorg* to a growing extent, and this cooperation was formalised at the beginning of 1945 under the label of HL.[9]

During the war, there had been a continuing debate on active/military versus passive/civilian resistance and the question of sabotage and guerrilla warfare. Military resistance was carried out by illegal groups, some Communist, and the British Special Operations Executive (SOE). In northern Norway, partisans did intelligence work and worked as agents for the Soviet Union. In drawing the line between legitimate and illegitimate organised resistance, the representations of the Communist resistance groups were especially important, since they had notably wanted a strategy of resistance that was in conflict with the approach taken by *Hjemmefronten* and the government in exile. *Kretsen* did not approve of *Milorg's* promotion of sabotage and armed resistance until the autumn of 1943.[10] *Hjemmefronten* as an organised unit was vulnerable to criticism of its social composition. In *Norges krig*, metaphors related to organisms are evoked to de-politicise the legitimate resistance movement. At the same time, Communist resistance is given a tenuous position in *Norges krig* and is written out of the past. This coincided with the growing vulnerability of the Communist party in Norwegian post-war society.

The different strategies adopted during the war not only gained their legitimacy during these five years – so that historians could be content to describe the development after the war – but the strategies also needed to be established as legitimate when the war ended. One of the other concerns in *Norges krig* was to constitute the difference between necessary adaptation and improper collaboration. The justification of *Administrasjonsrådet* (the Administrative Council) is a case in point. The Council was established by leading representatives of different government offices in the Oslo area in April 1940. Its main goal was to get the economic operations back on track and to return to normal in the occupied areas around the capital, even if this benefited the Germans. The Council was created at a time when Norwegian and German troops were still fighting in large parts of the country. Negotiations continued into the summer of 1940, but were overtaken by discussions about the planned *Riksråd*, a new Norwegian ruling body recognised by the occupation forces. Gunnar Jahn, a member of the Administrative Council himself and involved in the later negotiations, writes about the Council in *Norges krig* and depicts its creation as resulting from a sense of responsibility and an ability to think of society as a whole. Although the later negotiations over the *Riksråd* are presented as more blameworthy, still their main significance in *Norges krig* is not that many people in key positions set the constitution aside in an attempt to meet the demands of the German occupation forces, but that these later negotiations are rather presented as a starting-point for the resistance and thus inextricably connected to a growing Norwegian resistance.

In *Norges krig*, the murder of the deported Norwegian Jews in Auschwitz is described thus: 'Even a shocking tragedy such as this becomes only a detail in the abyss of brutality and cruelty the Germans demonstrated in their prisons.'[11] Norway's post-war memory culture brings to mind Pieter Lagrou's study of a patriotic interpretation of the occupation in early post-war Belgium, France and the Netherlands. His study specifically illustrates the precarious position reserved for the Jewish war experience within this patriotic memory culture. Immediately after the Second World War, the dominant image of the population of the concentration camps were those arrested for resistance, and the Jewish victims of genocide attracted less attention. In the construction of a 'fabricated universalism', the Jews were mixed with victims of other forms of persecution.[12] I will return to how the Norwegian public has dealt with the memory of the deportation of the Norwegian Jews, when I discuss the debates in the 1990s.

Norges krig employs ideas of participation and contribution, which have the potential of both including and excluding agents and actions. While women, for example, constitute a certain part of the broad national community in *Norges krig*, they are absent from a wide range of resistance activity, both civilian and military. At the same time, material damage is extensively portrayed in photographs where the inanimate victims of damage, the buildings, become the subject. Through a focus on the ruins, the previous inhabitants' gender, ethnicity and age as well as their social, political and economic circumstances are rendered invisible.[13] The ruined buildings which symbolise a collective experience, the plight of the Norwegian Jews, the broad definition of 'resistance', and the simultaneous naturalisation and de-politicising of the legitimate resistance movement can altogether be read as an inclination to create a uniform and collective war experience, leading to the construction of a homogeneous wartime community.

The Sustainability of the Grand Narrative since the 1950s

The first doctoral dissertations on wartime Norway were published at the end of the 1950s. One of the first three dealt with the military resistance movement, another looked at the question of Norway's government in the first five months of occupation, and a third examined the political role of the organisations.[14] What the studies had in common was that in different ways they all investigated occupied Norwegian society as an arena of political and strategic action. During the 1960s and 1970s, several works elaborated on different themes related to the main dichotomy between NS/the Germans and the Home Front/Norwegians in exile – with a keen eye to the resistance movement.[15]

In the 1970s, it becomes easier to discern an incipient critique of what were perceived as established historiographical perspectives. This critique evolved in two directions. Firstly, there was growing interest in the NS and its members, voiced by historians such as Hans Fredrik Dahl and then Guri Hjeltnes, Bernt Hagtvet, Øystein Sørensen, Tore Pryser and Nils Johan Ringdal.[16] Secondly, an increasing number of studies challenged dominant views on important themes in the history of the occupation, such as Lars Borgersrud's study of the reasons for the weaknesses of the Norwegian military campaign in 1940.[17] Other examples include Per Ole Johansen's work on the Jewish minority in Norway in the inter-war period and up to the deportation in the autumn of 1942, and Nils Johan Ringdal's book on the Norwegian police during the occupation.[18]

It has repeatedly been argued that there are forgotten groups and themes in the history of the occupation that deserve recognition and closer study. Such arguments can partly be linked to the growing focus on social history since the late 1960s. Througout the post-war era, there has been an increased willingness to pinpoint different, mainly civilian groups in Norwegian society and their fate during the war. In 1969, the teacher Oskar Mendelsohn published the first volume of his history of the Jews in Norway. The second volume came out in 1986, covering the period since the invasion in 1940.[19] Other examples of a turn toward social history are Guri Hjeltnes's work on everyday life during the occupation and her book, written together with Berit Nøkleby, on children in Norway during the war.[20] In another multi-volume work, Hjeltnes, Lauritz Pettersen, Bjørn Basberg and Atle Thowsen wrote the history of the Norwegian merchant fleet, which at the outbreak of the war was the fourth largest in the world.[21] The merchant fleet was requisitioned by the government in exile, to serve with the Allies. Sailors in the merchant navy made up the largest group of Norwegian war dead, and there was a lengthy controversy after the war about their entitlement to retroactive danger money.[22]

The connection between the historiography of the occupation and the Cold War is most obvious in topics such as Communist resistance and the Soviet military as an ally and liberator. The historians Lars Borgersrud, Terje Halvorsen and Torgrim Titlestad have been writing on issues related to the Communist resistance since the 1970s.[23] In the north of Norway, Finnmark was liberated by Soviet forces in the autumn of 1944. German military forces evacuated the population by force, leaving the country waste. The result of this scorched earth policy was suffering and hardship for the inhabitants of northern Norway for years after 1945. Starting from around 1970, this piece of war history was increasingly addressed by amateur historians and journalists.[24]

Challenging the Main Dichotomy

The first writings on the war appeared while Norway was still occupied. Not all of them were necessarily attempts to write history, but they can still be seen as starting points for different ways of writing and thinking about the war and its effects on Norwegian society. In this perspective, it is of course interesting to try to identify competing or alternative narratives of the occupation. Some writings have attempted to make adjustments to the main dichotomy, while others have challenged the polarity in more fundamental ways.

For example, the Administrative Council or the *Administrasjonsråd* has to a large extent been understood as representing a form of collaboration close to necessary adaptation, but the activities of many other groupings and agents who collaborated politically, socially or economically with the German occupation regime have been discredited after the war. The work by the writer Helge Krog which came to be known as *6-te kolonne?* started spreading in the Norwegian exile circles in Sweden during the war. It was further elaborated on and published in 1946, and is one of the earliest examples of a critique of economic collaboration and the unwillingness to sabotage those parts of Norwegian industry that provided raw material and products essential to German warfare. In February 1945, Krog wrote that it was the Norwegians' duty to try and hinder the export of such goods through determined sabotage: 'A one-day shortening of the war will save several thousand lives, Norwegian lives too', he argued.[25] Krog reasoned that the Germans had treated the organised resistance movement leniently during the occupation because the movement had abstained from determined sabotage. He thereby fundamentally challenged the perceived importance of the resistance movement. This perspective had little influence on the average historical representation of the war years, but public debates have subsequently been affected by ways of thinking which follow from Krog's analysis.

Even if Krog's perspective failed to influence later history writing, there are several examples of publications deemed so problematic by academic historians that they have sparked counterworks. In 1965, the British journalist Ralph Hewins published a biography entitled *Quisling – Prophet without Honour* to positive reviews in British and American papers as a revision of the traditional image of Quisling.[26] Leading Norwegian specialists on the war, however, voiced concern.[27] A year later, the book was translated into Norwegian by Hans S. Jacobsen, a National Socialist who had been in and out of NS during the 1930s and 1940s.[28] As a response aimed at international readers, the historians Olav Riste and Magne Skodvin collaborated with law professor Johs. Andenæs in writing *Norway and the Second World War*, which was published in 1966.[29] The foreword presents the book as an attempt to make the history of the occupation accessible to international readers, as they 'have had to rely on the occasional, often inadequate and sometimes distorting, accounts that have been published abroad'. While admitting that the publication was partly an initiative from the Ministry of Foreign Affairs, the authors claim that 'the book is in no way an "official version" of history – nor for that matter, does such a version exist.'[30]

The most obvious example of texts marginalised throughout the post-war era are the publications released by relentless former members of the NS. Out of a population of three million people at the outbreak of the war, 55,000 were members of the NS for varying lengths of time during the occupation. Their publications include books and the newspaper *Folk og Land* ('People and Country'). Even if these publications have been marginalized in public debate, several of the perspectives and arguments employed by NS and its members during the war have been circulating in the discourse on the war since the years of occupation. Some opinions are normally understood to have been held by a larger section of the population in 1940 than later in the war. That aside, the contributions from former NS members can be read as voices representing a marginalised discourse, yet some of these opinions, raised during the occupation and voiced by former NS members after the war, have provided arguments for books and debates on the memory of the war up until the present.

The argument that the politics of an inept and anti-militaristic reformist, Social Democratic, pre-war government led to a weakened military campaign following the German invasion is prominent in the post-war debates. In addition, the flight of the Social Democratic cabinet, led by Prime Minister Johan Nygaardsvold, into exile in the UK was already during the war referred to as treason in popular discourse. Furthermore, some have argued that it is problematic to claim that Norwegian citizens were obliged to follow guidelines from the exile government during the occupation. Both lines of argument carry the potential to undermine the legitimacy of *Hjemmefronten*, one fundamental element in the main dichotomy. Moreover, with reference to international law and the rights and responsibilities that the occupying forces have in securing an occupied area, the legitimacy of resistance work, armed resistance and the use of reprisals in occupied territory have been questioned, thus challenging the authority of the resistance. Another area of discussion concerns the terms of the capitulation in 1940 and the interrelated question of whether Norway was at war during the years of occupation. Like the previous argument, this line of reasoning similarly threatens to weaken the basis of the main dichotomy. This is what Johs. Andenæs says about the official view and its critics in *Norway and the Second World War*: 'It is now generally argued by former NS members and others affected by the judicial proceedings that the war came to an end at the time of the capitulation in northern Norway in June 1940.'[31] Andenæs discards the argument by pointing to the Norwegian Supreme Court's rejection of this interpretation in 1948, where the capitulation was understood as a military agreement relating to 'the surrender of the remaining Norwegian forces in northern Norway', and not as a general agreement between the two states Norway and Germany. Part of the discourse on the war, all these arguments can be invoked both by former members of the NS, journalists and historians.

As in Denmark, post-war Norwegian society has debated whether the outcome of the invasion was inevitable. During the Cold War, the primary moral lesson to be drawn from the Second World War was encapsulated in the slogan '*Aldri mer 9. april*' ('Never again 9 April'), which neatly served as an argument for stronger military defence and Norwegian membership of NATO. The anti-militaristic policies of the 1930s and the perceived failure to read the warning signs in the days leading up to the German invasion have been cited as a disappointment and a lesson learned for the protection of Norwegian post-war society. The critique of the failure of civil and military leaders to foresee the invasion and defend the nation is still quite pronounced in Norwegian public discourse on the war. Does this line of reasoning imply that under different circumstances, the Norwegian armed forces would have been able to fight back? In the absence of a comparative perspective, such notions ignore the fact that Norway was not the only European country overrun by Germany. A nationally framed understanding of the perceived Norwegian failure can thus be said to build on an implicit idea of Norwegian exceptionalism. As in the Finnish case, it points to a national tendency to view the involvement in European military conflicts as separate stories. The Battle of Narvik in the spring of 1940 is seldom brought up in these discussions, even if it is known internationally as one of the first setbacks for the German military forces during the war.

Three Historical Debates at the End of the Twentieth Century

Can events at the end of the Cold War be understood to have contributed to a potentially new understanding of the years of German occupation? The 1990s is arguably a possible turning-point in the transnational discourse on the Second World War. Certain key themes emerge, such as the German *Historikerstreit* of the 1980s and German unification; the question of the former East European nations' prospective membership of the European Union; the issue of reparations for past injustices; and the possibility that valuables stolen during the war were still kept in Swiss banks. The fate of the Jewish community of Europe – the Holocaust – is a common denominator. In Norway, three controversies in the 1980s and 1990s speak to a clash between different ways of looking at the past in light of these new events. I will argue that even if these controversies exemplify conflicting views on whether the history of the occupation should be understood in a national or a transnational context, a nationally framed understanding of the occupation has held a leading position throughout the post-war era into the twenty-first century.

A Norwegian Historikerstreit

In 1989, the historian Øystein Sørensen claimed that the main problem in the previous historical studies of the years of occupation was tied to the historian's dual role as both participant and observer.[32] According to Sørensen, the research from the 1950s – supervised by Sverre Steen – was comparative and open, while from the 1960s on – under leadership of Magne Skodvin – the research was narrowed down both thematically, methodically and in terms of perspective and ideology. Attention was given to the work of the resistance, while the 'NS and the occupation forces were downgraded' to such an extent that it was appropriate to call it neglect.[33]

Sørensen and the historian Nils Johan Ringdal were interviewed later in 1989 in the newspaper *Aftenposten*, under the heading 'the new *Historikerstreit*'.[34] They were introduced as a new generation of researchers on the occupation, who found it just as acceptable to collect their sources at the *Institutt for norsk okkupasjonshistorie*, led by former NS members, as at Norway's Resistance Museum *Hjemmefrontmuseet*. Sørensen and Ringdal emphasised the need for history writing on the members and representatives of the NS and the German occupiers. In this perspective, a rewriting of the history of the occupation was needed because the former members of the NS had been met with a judgmental and moralising attitude from earlier historians. Furthermore, 'distance' was a key word for Sørensen and Ringdal. To some extent, their position resembles Martin Broszat's argument for a historicisation of the Nazi period: there was a need to treat the Nazi regime as any other historical phenomenon. To be able to do this required historical distance.[35]

The Norwegian case illustrates how the West German *Historikerstreit* was creolised to fit into a nationally framed understanding of the war. The German debate dealt with the writing and potential rewriting of the history of Nazism and its crimes, but the *Historikerstreit* also had to do with the potential rehabilitation of Germany's national past. Some of the contributors to the German debate emphasised the need for a more positive German national identity separated from the atrocities of the past. One might ask if the national scope and frame of the study of Norway during the war was reinforced rather than fundamentally challenged by the contribution from Sørensen and Ringdal. In insisting that historians needed to focus their attention on the NS and the occupiers, the two historians in their own way reinforced the idea of a polarised wartime community and confirmed that an important dividing line was still to be drawn between the former members of the NS and the rest of society. Moreover, the focus on the NS and the German occupiers was not primarily deemed necessary because of the need to identify the perpetrators or establish Norwegian responsibility for the atrocities of the past. Even if the target was the collaborators and National Socialists, the concepts of 'perpetrators, victims and bystanders', terms central to the German debate, were left untouched. Topics such as Norwegian volunteers for the German–Soviet war and joint responsibility for the genocide in arresting and deporting Norwegian Jews were not highlighted.[36] The creolisation of the ongoing transnational debate thus seemed to imply that the Norwegian community had been unaffected by the atrocities that were crucial in the *Historikerstreit*.

Restitution for the Norwegian Jews

The executive committee of the World Jewish Congress met in Oslo in the autumn of 1996 to discuss their international work in examining where the German confiscations of Jewish property and belongings during the Second World War were deposited. By this juncture, a Norwegian investigating committee had already been appointed, charged with mapping out what was done with the property and possessions confiscated from the Norwegian Jews and how the settlements after the war had been carried out.[37] County governor Oluf Skarpnes was appointed chairman of the committee; other members were the academic historians Bjarte Bruland, Eli Fure (from the National Archives) and Professor Ole Kristian Grimnes from the University of Oslo. Additional members were Professor Thor Falkanger from the same university's Faculty of Law, district court judge Guri Sunde and psychologist Berit Reisel. Reisel and Bruland were the appointed representatives of the Mosaic Religious Community (the Jewish communities of Oslo and Trondheim). At the time, Bruland had recently completed his master's thesis on the attempt to exterminate the Norwegian Jews.[38]

A few days before the committee were to make its conclusions public at a press conference in June 1997, news of a divided statement reached the media. The minority consisting of Bruland and Reisel was objecting, while the historians Grimnes and Fure were part of the majority. A fundamental dividing line had emerged around the issue of context: the majority thought the relevant framework to be national, arguing that the case of the Norwegian Jews had to be seen in light of the losses suffered by *all* Norwegians and that Norwegian society was in no state to provide a more generous economic settlement after the war:

> [...] a good and thorough process of compensation and return was carried out after the war. But the Norwegian society was economically stripped, at the same time as it faced enormous expenses for rebuilding the country [...] It was not economically possible to give full compensation, either to Jews or non-Jewish Norwegians, for what they had lost during the war. The nation in its entirety had lost. Individual citizens also had to put up with starting the post-war period with economic losses and reduced welfare.[39]

Drawing on international historical research on the Holocaust, the minority argued that the war experience of the Jewish minority could not be compared to the experiences of non-Jewish Norwegians. The fate of the Norwegian Jews had to be understood in relation to the Nazi attempt to liquidate the Jews both economically and physically.

In light of the national historiographical traditions in dealing with this topic, the minority's contribution to the report and the following debate represented a challenge to the traditional national narrative. In the narratives about the arrest of the Norwegian Jews in *Norges krig* and *Norge i krig* it is clear that a national and patriotic narrative can hardly accommodate both the Norwegian police officers as the subjects who made the arrests and Jewish people as the objects who were arrested.[40] In such narratives, it is possible to write about human tragedies without drawing attention to the ones who took active part in these actions. Such narrative patterns also tend to position the victims as the objects of both the author's and the reader's evaluation. For example, *Norge i krig* states that 'it is characteristic that the Jews, who were arrested to be taken away, did not protest or fight back.'[41] In the *Norsk krigsleksikon* from 1995, police involvement in the various attempts to register the Norwegian Jews prior to their arrest and deportation as well as their participation in these actions are described using the reference word '*jødeaksjonene*', actions against the Jews. The text explicitly states that the arrests of male Jews were carried out by state police and groups of ordinary Norwegian policemen.[42] In several ways, this text marks a clean break from the portrayal in the earlier works of the arrest and deportation of Norwegian Jews, making the 1990s a potential turning-point.

For some, the point of having historians appointed as members of investigative committees must be to establish 'what actually happened'. After the war, when official Norway was forced to review its policy against its Jewish citizens, most members of the Norwegian investigating committee, including representatives from the Norwegian community of historians, failed to understand that times had indeed changed. Leading politicians from across the political spectrum sided with the minority: the 'past' as it was represented by the professional historians of the majority report was vetoed when the politicians entered the stage. Parliament decided to grant collective compensation to the Mosaic Religious Community. Part of this restitution was invested in establishing the Centre for Studies of Holocaust and Religious Minorities in Oslo.

Debating David Irving

In the summer of 1996, the British writer David Irving sued American academic Deborah Lipstadt for libel. Lipstadt had identified Irving as a Holocaust denier in her book *Denying the Holocaust*, published in 1993.[43] Around the same time, in the Norwegian newspaper *Dagbladet*, the Norwegian historian Hans Fredrik Dahl commented on the decision made by the American publishing house St. Martin's Press not to publish Irving's biography of Goebbels.[44] Dahl described Irving's book as a 'scholarly work from the leading source critic on the history of Nazism today', stating that he had read the biography and could 'guarantee its high professional quality'.[45] As professor of media studies at the University of Oslo, author of several works on the history of the occupation and a long-time contributor to the *Dagbladet* (including several years as the paper's cultural editor), Dahl's position in Norwegian public debate was not to be underestimated.

Dahl's positive assessment of Irving's work as a historian generated a huge debate in a number of Norwegian newspaper, with contributions from several academics and journalists. One of the issues at stake was the line Dahl drew between Irving as a political figure (of the extreme right) and his work as a historian. There were many who argued against such a segregation of history and politics, especially in dealing with the phenomenon of revisionism and outright Holocaust denial. Could someone like Irving be praised for his historical writing?

In his *Kampen mot glemselen* ('The fight against oblivion') published in 1997, historian Odd-Bjørn Fure analysed Irving's biography of Goebbels and other writings, with a special focus on Irving's analysis of the extermination of the Jews.[46] Fure's book was also a thorough critique of the perceived tendencies in Dahl's commentaries on wartime Norway more generally, claiming that in printing Dahl's pieces, *Dagbladet* had shown a severe lack of historical consciousness. Several of Dahl's pieces, Fure argued, showed a tendency to 'minimise the crimes of the Nazi State and embellish the German occupation of Norway'.[47] Fure quoted Dahl's commentary in *Dagbladet* in May 1995 on the occasion of the fiftieth anniversary of the liberation: Dahl claimed that with the exception of what in his estimate were about 0.3% of the population – sailors in the Merchant Navy, volunteers in the German–Soviet war and soldiers under Allied command – no Norwegians had been at war. Furthermore:

> [...] those 5,000 courageous, heroic youths of the resistance [...] voluntarily chose a guerrilla stance against the superior forces [and] lived of course in self-inflicted mortal danger. But mother and father and the rest of the population did not. The German forces in Norway showed through most of these five years no small sense of self-control toward the passively reluctant population. They were polite, correct, well-organised; an occupation force many countries throughout history would have envied us.[48]

Dahl evokes an image of a polarised Norwegian community where the occupiers were not as harmful as historians have portrayed them and where the majority – the passively reluctant – are constructed as a homogenous collective. In claiming that no members of the Norwegian community were really at risk during the occupation other than those who voluntarily chose to inflict mortal danger on themselves, Dahl makes Jews and political opponents of National Socialism disappear from history. Some have declared Dahl the *enfant terrible* of Norwegian occupation historiography. In a possible attempt to challenge the patriotic narrative, Dahl ends up producing a caricature, undressing the heroes, transforming the aggressors into gentlemen of remarkable restraint and leaving the victims out. The issue of what was at stake during the Second World War collapses. In such a representation, National Socialism is not an ideology eradicating democracy and human lives through genocide, nor is the war understood as total war.

The Norwegian controversy about Irving was not first and foremost about the history of the German occupation of Norway. Yet Fure's analysis functioned as a prism, highlighting important aspects found both in Dahl's writings and in the practices of the media. Moreover, Fure also observed that professional historians were absent from the debate preceding Dahl's appraisal of Irving. Fure therefore described the situation as 'a vacuum of knowledge in media society', although it is difficult to agree wholeheartedly with him on this in hindsight.[49] His own contribution, along with the input of several younger historians and journalists in the Irving debate, voiced a willingness to integrate international historical discourses and viewpoints in Norwegian public debate.

Conclusion

In 1995, the year of the fiftieth anniversary of the liberation, the cultural historian Anne Eriksen published her study *Det var noe annet under krigen* ('It was different during the war'). She identified the basic or fundamental story about the years of occupation as presented in popular memories, anniversaries, museums and books. This narrative superstructure for Eriksen highlighted the importance of an inclusive definition of resistance and what she calls the 'mythologising of the war', a process where the past is naturalised and depoliticised.[50] Also, her work mainly focuses on the role played by the members of the NS and the German occupiers as enemies of the nation. Eriksen devotes less attention to other 'out-groups', such as the role ascribed to the Norwegian Jews within the national narrative. Eriksen's work was an important contribution to the study of the years of occupation and launched a wave of memory studies dealing with the Second World War.[51]

At the outset, I underlined that 'the War' has embodied varying values for different agents at different points in time. A nationally framed understanding appears consistent over time, but ought to be conceived of as relying on changing contexts. While the 1990s can be said to constitute a potential turning-point in a transnational discourse on the war, the three Norwegian controversies in the 1980s and 1990s reveal the conflicting views on whether the history of the occupation is best understood in a national or a transnational context. Even if the historiography of the post-war period testifies to a wealth of research topics and perspectives, the controversies discussed here also show that it is difficult to claim that professional historians by themselves have challenged a nationally framed understanding of the occupation. On the contrary, leading Norwegian historians have more-or-less implicitly conceptualised wartime Norway as a homogenous society, making the nation-state the given scene for debates on war memory. In the last twenty years, sources that used to be unattainable have increasingly become available, enabling new studies and debates.[52] There is multi-faceted research on topics connected to the war, reflecting post-war historiographical developments in the growing fragmentation and specialisation of the discipline of history. When looking at the developments in both the historiography and memory culture since the mid 1990s, it is possible to claim that several historical works and projects have taken up the study of previously neglected or controversial themes that have the potential to challenge a national framework. At the same time, recent developments in the memory culture as it has been expressed in public debates and films seem to have reinforced an understanding of the war which continues to be nationally framed.

Notes

1 Stefan Berger & Chris Lorenz (eds.), *The Contested Nation: Ethnicity, Class, Religion and Gender in National Histories* (Basingstoke, 2008).

2 'Etterkrigstidens nasjonale fortelling om okkupasjonstiden kom til å bli spunnet omkring denne motsetningen: Okkupasjonshistorien fikk en grunnstruktur.' Ole Kristian Grimnes, 'Hvor står okkupasjons-historien nå?', *Nytt Norsk Tidsskrift*, 2009:3/4.

3 Odd-Bjørn Fure, 'Norsk okkupasjonshistorie: Konsensus, berøringsangts og tabuisering', in: Stein Ugelvik Larsen (ed.), *I krigens kjølvann: Nye sider ved norsk krigshistorie og etterkrigstid* (Oslo, 1999).

4 In the early 1950s, Nils Christie argued in his dissertation that the Norwegian prison guards at the Norwegian concentration camps for foreign prisoners were no less brutal than the guards in European camps. See Nils Christie, *Fangevoktere i konsentrasjonsleire: En sosiologisk undersøkelse* (Oslo, 1952).

5 By amateur historians I mean all those writers of history who do not have a degree in history. For historiographical overviews, see Øystein Sørensen, 'Forskningen om krigen i Norge: Tradisjonelle og nye perspektiver', *Nytt Norsk Tidsskrift*, 1989:1; Ole Kristian Grimnes, 'Historieskrivingen om okkupasjonen', *Nytt Norsk Tidsskrift*, 1990:2; Berit Nøkleby, 'Okkupasjonshistorien – et minefelt', in: Henrik G. Bastiansen, Bernt Hagtvet, Knut Lundby, Helge Rønning & Guri Hjeltnes (eds.), *Det elegante uromoment: Hans Fredrik Dahl og offentligheten* (Oslo, 2009); Synne Corell, *Krigens ettertid: Okkupasjonshistorien i norske historiebøker* (Oslo, 2011).

6 Ideally a historiographical study of the different discourses on the occupation would shift the focus beyond the classification of texts into certain genres and disciplines to an attempt to look at the interplay between the diverse texts which represent knowledge and make statements about the occupation.

7 Sivert Langholm, 'The Infrastructure of History', in: William H. Hubbard, Jan Eivind Myhre, Trond Nordby & Sølvi Sogner (eds.), *Making a Historical Culture: Historiography in Norway* (Oslo, 1995), 99.

8 Sverre Steen (ed.), *Norges krig*, 3 vols. (Oslo, 1947–1950); Magne Skodvin (ed.), *Norge i krig*, 8 vols. (Oslo, 1984–1987); Hans Fredrik Dahl, Guri Hjeltnes, Berit Nøkleby, Nils Johan Ringdal & Øystein Sørensen (eds.), *Norsk krigsleksikon 1940–45* (Oslo, 1995).

9 Ole Kristian Grimnes, 'Hjemmefrontens ledelse (HL)', in: Hans Fredrik Dahl, Guri Hjeltnes, Berit Nøkleby, Nils Johan Ringdal & Øystein Sørensen (eds.), *Norsk krigsleksikon 1940–45* (Oslo, 1995).

10 See Olav Njølstad, *Jens Chr. Hauge – fullt og helt* (Oslo, 2008), 158.

11 'Selv en så rystende tragedie som denne blir likevel bare en detalj i den avgrunn av brutalitet og råskap som tyskerne viste i sine fengsler.' Haakon Holmboe, 'De som ble tatt', in: Sverre Steen (ed.), *Norges krig*, vol. III (Oslo, 1950), 488.

12 Pieter Lagrou, 'Victims of Genocide and National Memory: Belgium, France and the Netherlands 1945–1965', *Past and Present*, 1997:154, 183, 184, 186 and 196.

13 Elizabeth Heineman, 'The Hour of the Woman: Memories of Germany's "Crisis Years" and West German National Identity', *The American Historical Review*, 1996:101/2, 368.

14 Sverre Kjeldstadli, *Hjemmestyrkene: Hovedtrekk av den militære motstanden under okkupasjonen* (Oslo, 1959); Magne Skodvin, *Striden om okkupasjonsstyret i Norge fram til 25. september 1940* (Oslo, 1956); Thomas Chr. Wyller, *Nyordning og motstand: En framstilling og en analyse av organisasjonenes politiske funksjon under den tyske okkupasjonen 25.9.1940–25.9.1942* (Oslo, 1958).

15 See, for instance, Olav Riste, *'London-regjeringa': Norge i krigsalliansen 1940–1945*, 2. vols., (Oslo, 1973–1979); Ole Kristian Grimnes, *Et flyktningesamfunn vokser fram: Nordmenn i Sverige 1940–45* (Oslo, 1969); Ole Kristian Grimnes, *Hjemmefrontens ledelse* (Oslo, 1977); Olav Riste & Berit Nøkleby, *Norway 1940–45: The Resistance Movement* (Oslo, 1970).

16 Hans Fredrik Dahl, 'Norsk politikk 1940–1945: Kontinuitet eller brudd?', *Kontrast*, 1971:25; Hans Fredrik Dahl, *Krigen i Norge* (Oslo, 1974); Hans Fredrik Dahl, *'Dette er London': NRK i krig 1940–1945* (Oslo, 1978); Hans Fredrik Dahl & Tom B. Jensen, *Parti og plakat: NS 1933–1945* (Oslo, 1988); Øystein Sørensen, *Fra Marx til Quisling: Fem sosialisters vei til NS* (Oslo, 1983); Øystein Sørensen, *Hitler eller Quisling?: Ideologiske brytninger i Nasjonal samling 1940–1945* (Oslo, 1989); Øystein Sørensen, *Solkors og solidaritet: Høyreautoritær samfunnstenkning i Norge ca. 1930–1945* (Oslo, 1991); Rolf Fladby & Tore Pryser, *Bygd og by under okkupasjonen* (Oslo, 1982); Tore Pryser, *Arbeiderbevegelsen og Nasjonal samling: Om venstrestrømninger i Quislings parti NS* (Oslo, 1991); Guri Hjeltnes, Hans Fredrik Dahl & Bernt Hagtvet, *Den*

norske nasjonalsosialismen: Nasjonal Samling 1933–1945 i tekst og bilder (Oslo, 1982).

17 Lars Borgersrud, 'Nye momenter til forståelse av moderne norsk krigshistorie: Trekk ved den militærpolitiske utviklinga i Norge 1918–40, og begrensninger de la på den norske krigføringa i 1940' (M.A. diss.; Bergen, 1975); Lars Borgersrud, *'Unngå å irritere fienden–': Krigen i Norge 1940: Eventyr og virkelighet* (Oslo, 1981).

18 Per Ole Johansen, *Oss selv nærmest: Norge og jødene 1914–1943* (Oslo, 1984); Nils Johan Ringdal, *Mellom barken og veden: Politiet under okkupasjonen* (Oslo, 1987).

19 Oskar Mendelsohn, *Jødenes historie i Norge gjennom 300 år*, 2 vols. (Oslo, 1969 & 1986).

20 Guri Hjeltnes, *Hverdagsliv i krig: Norge 1940–45* (Oslo, 1987); Guri Hjeltnes & Berit Nøkleby, *Barn under krigen* (Oslo, 2000).

21 *Handelsflåten i krig 1939–1945*, 5 vols. (Oslo, 1992–1997).

22 In addition to the controversy over retroactive danger money, there has been criticism of the Norwegian government's practice of granting war pensions not only to sailors in the merchant fleet but to several other groups as well. Even if this practice can be said to reflect the importance attached to the different contributions to the war effort by post-war officialdom, I have chosen not to elaborate on this question.

23 Lars Borgersrud, *Wollweber-organisasjonen i Norge* (Oslo, 1995); Lars Borgersrud, *Fiendebilde Wollweber: Svart propaganda i kald krig* (Oslo, 2001); Terje Halvorsen, *Mellom Moskva og Berlin: Norges kommunistiske parti under ikke-angrepspakten mellom Sovjet-Unionen og Tyskland 23. august 1939–22. juni 1941* (Oslo, 1996); Terje Halvorsen, 'Okkupasjonshistorien og de besværlige kommunistene', in: *Fagbevegelsen som etterkrigshistorisk forskningsfelt*, 'Etterkrigshistorisk register', vol. XIII (Bergen, 1999); Torgrim Titlestad, 'NKP mellom nasjonale og internasjonale straumdrag 1939–1941' (M.A. diss.; Bergen, 1973); Torgrim Titlestad, *Stalin midt imot: Peder Furubotn 1938–41* (Oslo, 1977); Torgrim Titlestad, *I kamp, i krig: Peder Furubotn 1942–45* (Oslo, 1977); Torgrim Titlestad, *Frihetskampen i Norge: Og historikerne som sviktet* (Oslo, 2010).

24 Jørn W. Ruud, 'Erindringen om andre verdenskrig i Finnmark og Nord-Troms' (M.A. diss.; Bergen, 2008), 8–9 in particular.

25 Helge Krog, *6-te kolonne?* (Oslo, 1946), 29.

26 Ralph Hewins, *Quisling – Prophet without Honour* (London, 1965).

27 Hans Fredrik Dahl, 'Hewins-saken', in: Hans Fredrik Dahl, Guri Hjeltnes, Berit Nøkleby, Nils Johan Ringdal & Øystein Sørensen (eds.), *Norsk krigsleksikon 1940–45* (Oslo, 1995).

28 Øystein Sørensen, 'Jacobsen, Hans S.', in: Hans Fredrik Dahl, Guri Hjeltnes, Berit Nøkleby, Nils Johan Ringdal & Øystein Sørensen (eds.), *Norsk krigsleksikon 1940–45* (Oslo, 1995).

29 Johs. Andenæs, Olav Riste & Magne Skodvin, *Norway and the Second World War* (Oslo, 1966).

30 Olav Riste, 'Foreword', in: Johs. Andenæs, Olav Riste & Magne Skodvin, *Norway and the Second World War* (Oslo, 1966).

31 Johs. Andenæs, 'The Post-War Proceedings against Enemy Collaborators', in: Johs. Andenæs, Olav Riste & Magne Skodvin, *Norway and the Second World War* (Oslo, 1966), 135–136.

32 Sørensen 1989, 40.

33 'Nasjonal Samling og okkupasjonsmakten er blitt så sterkt nedprioritert at man med få unntak kan snakke om en ren neglisjering' (Sørensen 1989, 45).

34 'Den nye historiker-striden', *Aftenposten*, 20 December, 1989.

35 Saul Friedländer, *Memory, History and the Extermination of the Jews of Europe* (Bloomington, 1993); Martin Broszat & Saul Friedländer, 'A Controversy about the Historicization of National Socialism', *New German Critique*, 1988:44, 85–126.

36 Sørensen's list of new perspectives and specific topics for further study did not include questions related to perpetrators, victims and bystanders. Anti-Semitism and ideas about race were connected to NS ideology and politics. Øystein Sørensen, 'Forskningen om krigen i Norge. Tradisjonelle og nye perspektiver', *Nytt Norsk Tidsskrift*, 1989:1. In an interview in *Aftenposten*, Sørensen asked: 'What was the extermination of the Jews other than fanatical and extreme ideas put to life?' while Ringdal stated: '[...] I have personally gone much further than many other Norwegian historians in the attempt to elucidate the small share of responsibility that rests on Norwegian shoulders. [...] I was very concerned about the contribution of the police in the Jewish question in Norway. But my conclusion was that you cannot accuse the police of anything other than participation in sending the Jews out of the country. They had no responsibility for the extermination as such.' 'Den nye historiker-striden', *Aftenposten*, 20 December, 1989.

37 NOU 1997:22, *Inndragning av jødisk eiendom i Norge under den 2. verdenskrig*, 11.

38 Bjarte Bruland, 'Forsøket på å tilintetgjøre de norske jødene' (M.A. diss.; Bergen, 1995).

39 '[...] det ble utført et godt og grundig tilbakeførings- og erstatningsoppgjør etter krigen. Men det norske samfunn var økonomisk ribbet, samtidig som det sto overfor enorme utgifter til gjenreisning av landet [...] Det var ikke økonomisk mulig å yte full erstatning, hverken til jøder eller ikke-jødiske nordmenn, for hva de hadde tapt under krigen. Nasjonen som helhet hadde tapt. Da måtte også de enkelte borgere finne seg i å begynne etterkrigstiden med økonomiske tap og nedsatt velferd'. NOU 1997:22, *Inndragning av jødisk eiendom i Norge under den 2. verdenskrig*, 13.

40 The Norwegian police were in a unique position during the occupation because they could arrest their fellow citizens on behalf of the NS and the occupiers, and could also be arrested themselves. The police were soon asked to enroll in the NS. More than 40 per cent did. At the same time, several police officers actively participated in illegal action.

41 'Men det er karakteristisk at jøder som ble arrestert for å føres bort, ikke

protesterte eller satte seg til motverge'. Tim Greve, *Verdenskrig, Norge i krig*, vol. 3 (Oslo, 1985), 125.

42 Per Ole Johansen, 'Jødeaksjonene', in: Hans Fredrik Dahl, Guri Hjeltnes, Berit Nøkleby, Nils Johan Ringdal & Øystein Sørensen (eds.), *Norsk krigsleksikon 1940–45* (Oslo, 1995).

43 Deborah E. Lipstadt, *Denying the Holocaust: The Growing Assault on Truth and Memory* (New York, 1993).

44 David Irving, *Goebbels: Mastermind of the Third Reich* (London, 1996).

45 'et vitenskapelig arbeid fra den fremste kildekritiker innen nazismens historie i dag'; 'jeg har lest biografien, og kan innestå for dens faglige kvalitet'. Hans Fredrik Dahl, 'Sår som ikke gror', *Dagbladet*, 25 June 1996.

46 Odd-Bjørn Fure, *Kampen mot glemselen: Kunnskapsvakuum i mediesamfunnet* (Oslo, 1997).

47 Fure 1997, 29.

48 '[...] de fem tusen dristige, motstandsbevegelsens heltemodige ungdommer [...] valgte en frivillig geriljastand mot denne overmakt, levde selvfølgelig i egenforskyldt livsfare. Men mor og far og befolkningen ellers gjorde det ikke. De tyske styrkene i Norge viste gjennom størstedelen av de fem årene ikke liten selvbeherskelse overfor den passivt motvillige befolkningen. De var høflige, korrekte, vel organiserte; en okkupasjonsmakt mange land gjennom historien ville misunt oss.' Hans Fredrik Dahl, 'Seier'n på norsk', *Dagbladet*, 7 July 1995, quoted in Fure 1997, 30–31.

49 The title of Fure's book translates as 'The fight against oblivion: A vacuum of knowledge in the media society'.

50 Anne Eriksen, *Det var noe annet under krigen* (Oslo, 1995), 49 and 145.

51 Eriksen's work and the project 'The Development of Norwegian National Identity in the Nineteenth Century' carried out at the University of Oslo in the 1990s, are two examples of Norwegian studies connected to the international interest in collective memory and national identities which began in the 1980s. In addition to Eriksen's work, five relatively new dissertations have in different ways focused on the narratives of the German occupation. There are also several studies of the narratives of the occupation in Norwegian school textbooks. See Claudia Lenz, *Von der patriotischen Pflicht, das Haus in Ordnung zu halten: Bedeutungswandel innerhalb der individuellen und kollektiven Erinnerung an den Widerstand norwegischer Frauen gegen die deutsche Besatzung nach 1945* (Hamburg, 2002); Clemens Maier, *Making Memories: The Politics of Remembrance in Postwar Norway and Denmark* (Florence, 2007); Anette Storeide, *Fortellingen om fangenskapet* (Oslo, 2007); Susanne Maerz, *Die langen Schatten der Besatzungszeit: 'Vergangenheitsbewältigung' in Norwegen als Identitetätsdiskurs* (Berlin, 2008); Corell 2011. For the narratives of the occupation in Norwegian school textbooks, see Kristin Mikalsen, 'Historieformidling og oppdragelse: Nazisme og andre verdenskrig i norske og tyske lærebøker i historie fra 1950-tallet til i dag' (M.A. diss.; Tromsø, 2007); Bjørn Anders Skarsem, 'Andre verdenskrig i lærebøker for gymnaset/den videregående skolen' (M.A. diss.; Trondheim, 2007).

52 Tore Pryser, *Fra varm til kald krig: Etterretningskuppet på Lillehammer i frigjøringsdagene 1945 og et mulig mord* (Oslo, 1994); Tore Pryser, *Kvinner i hemmelige tjenester: Etterretning i Norden under den annen verdenskrig* (Oslo, 2007); Tore Pryser, *Hitlers hemmelige agenter: Tysk etterretning i Norge 1939–1945* (Oslo, 2001); Kristin Hatledal, 'Krigsheltinne eller tyskarjente?: Historia om Dagmar Lahlum – i lys av andre etterretningskvinner' (M.A. diss.; Oslo, 2009). The author Vibeke Løkkeberg initiated a debate on the allied bombing of Bergen in a recent novel. See Vibeke Løkkeberg, *Allierte* (Oslo, 2007).

CHAPTER 6

The Rise and Fall of Small-State Realism

Sweden and the Second World War

Johan Östling

In the eyes of its inhabitants, post-war Sweden was by all accounts a unique country. With its peaceful, evolutionary character, the course of modern Swedish history was certainly very different from the brutal developments on the European Continent. Much of this was thanks to the simple fact that Sweden, as one of few major European countries, had been spared the horrors of the Second World War. At the same time, the Swedish narratives of the war underwent a post-1945 transformation that held close to wider European currents, particularly after the late 1980s. In an international perspective, the neutral democracy of the North is therefore especially interesting.[1]

The Swedish case also stands out in various ways in the Nordic framework. In contrast to her neighbours, Sweden had not been directly affected by the war through occupation, bombing or devastation. The year 1945 did not mark an absolute turning-point in Swedish history, and Sweden remained neutral in the Cold War. Moreover, since the early 1990s, the controversies seem to have been more passionate and the assault on the dominant post-war narrative more fundamental than in the other Nordic countries.[2]

Small-State Realism

The aftermath of the war was far less turbulent for Sweden than for many other countries. With the exception of a few minor trials, no legal action was taken against former Nazis. Given that there was no resistance movement set on monopolising the interpretation of the war, and no occupying power to dictate post-war conditions, it becomes clearer why the Second World War never really became part of the official national memory.[3]

Despite this, in the late 1940s, a powerful narrative of Sweden and the Second World War did emerge, a hegemonic interpretation that was to dominate the entire post-war era. It may best be characterised as the *small-state realistic narrative*. Being a small state, the argument went, Sweden had no choice but to tailor her responses to aggressive German power. This much was undisputed in the dominant Swedish interpretation. However, it was held that Sweden's concessions had been limited, and the price paid – having to acquiesce in the face of Nazi aggression – was seen as stemming directly from the threat of occupation. Sweden's policy of neutrality had thus been to the lasting benefit of the nation, her neighbours, and peace itself. 'The role of a small state gave Sweden moral absolution,' as the historian Alf W. Johansson wrote in the mid 1990s in a paradigmatic article on small-state realism and Swedish self-image:

> All the difficult questions which the policy of concessions posed about the Swedish social ethos during the war years, about the will to resist and submission, about fidelity to one's own ideals and ideological principles, were swept under the carpet by the triumph of small-state realism.[4]

Small-state realism was at the core of Sweden's national identity in the post-war period. As in many other European countries, its hegemonic phase coincided with the Cold War years. Self-righteousness was a salient feature. Admittedly, Sweden had in some ways deviated from strict neutrality, but on the whole the Swedish policy had been that of resistance and a major effort for peace. 'We have made our contribution, we have struggled in our own way', the Swedish Prime Minister Per Albin Hansson concluded in a speech on the very last day of the war. To his mind his wartime coalition government not only had acted successfully but that the whole social order and Swedish way of life was superior.[5]

The structure of the small-state realistic narrative also required a set of scapegoats. The most obvious culprits were the Quislings and the fifth columnists, that is, Swedish Nazis and Communists, whose dubious loyalties made them potential traitors. The other group of whipping-boys consisted of the candid opponents of National Socialism in publishing, culture and intellectual debate, including Torgny Segerstedt, Ture Nerman and Karl Gerhard. Their in official eyes treacherous, overstrung animosity towards government policy cast them as conceited idealists who threatened to bring Sweden into war.

The need for a unifying memory of the war was not as urgent in Sweden as it was in many European countries. The small-state realistic narrative nevertheless served to underpin and strengthen national traditions in post-war Sweden. For example, criticism of wartime small-state realism amounted to criticism of Cold War small-state realism. This is not contradicted by the idea – suggested, for example, by the historian Bo Stråth – that neutrality was in part a construction after the event, and that the doctrine itself did not take shape until the beginning of the 1950s. At the heart of the small-state realistic narrative was a plea for the fundamental principles in post-war Swedish society: peace and security; sovereignty and neutrality; welfare, modernity and progress.[6]

Despite the lack of obvious heroism, the Swedish narrative comprised elements similar to those of other European countries. Small-state realism could be regarded as a 'progressive narrative', where the evil of National Socialism was located in a historical epoch now firmly in the past. By such means, the coalition government seemed a stable guarantor of peace and sovereignty, and its policy of neutrality had spared Sweden war and occupation.[7]

Furthermore, Sweden's humanitarian efforts in war-torn Europe were emphasised, a proud and important tradition which continued in the reconstruction of the Continent after 1945 and in an ever-increasing international commitment in the 1950s and 1960s. In a curious but significant way, Swedish small-state realism could be smoothly combined with a kind of *small-state idealism*, where Sweden, as a neutral and peaceful democracy, could act on the international scene.

As a dominant narrative, the small-state realistic interpretation recurred whenever the theme of Sweden and the Second World

War cropped up. This was the background to the memoirs and biographies published in Sweden, and the perspective permeated textbooks, films and television series.[8] Some of the flavour – and impact – of small-state realism is best described by focusing on its paradigmatic position in post-war academic historiography.

A Historiographical Paradigm

After a short period of intense debate in the immediate post-war period, Swedish memories of the Second World War faded fast.[9] Only a handful of significant books were published in the 1950s and 1960s, and academic interest was almost non-existent.

The majority of the more substantial contributions made to the history of Sweden during the Second World War were written in the spirit of small-state realism. In 1958, for instance, the senior diplomat Gunnar Hägglöf published a book on Swedish trade policy toward both Germany and the Allies. Hägglöf, himself one of the key wartime negotiators, described the policy as a balancing act, without discussing the moral dilemma of Sweden's exports of iron ore to Nazi Germany. Four years later the historian Åke Thulstrup wrote a book on German attempts to influence Swedish public opinion in 1933 to 1945. Although actively engaged in anti-Nazi circles during the war, Thulstrup's overall assessment of Sweden's actions was not particularly harsh. As with the school textbooks and general histories of the period, the paradigm of Thulstrup's account was *Realpolitik*.[10]

In the 1970s and 1980s, by contrast, research on Sweden and the Second World War gained momentum. Historiography was pervaded by small-state realism, which buttressed most of the studies and shaped the overall scholarly debate. This period is very much associated with a large research project at the Department of History in Stockholm, 'Sverige under andra världskriget' (SUAV; 'Sweden during the Second World War'). Within this project, some twenty doctoral theses were published in the 1970s. A whole range of new empirical fields was analysed, with an emphasis on political, economic and social history.[11]

Back in the late 1960s, the historian Wilhelm M. Carlgren, head of the Swedish Ministry for Foreign Affairs' archive, had been commissioned by the government to write a history of Swedish foreign policy during the Second World War. His 600-page book, *Svensk utrikespolitik 1939–1945* (1973; 'Swedish Foreign Policy 1939–1945'), is a thorough but respectful study that benefited from his outstanding command of the diplomatic and political sources. Although he touched on the moral issues, his fundamental assumption was that the military threat from Germany was a real one, and must be considered when judging Sweden's concessions. On the whole, Carlgren showed a far-reaching understanding of Swedish foreign policy during the war, and many of the politicians responsible were depicted with sympathy. His *magnum opus* is an impressive monument to small-state realism, the historiographical paradigm of his day.[12]

Young researchers within the SUAV project did not have the same free access to the archives Carlgren had enjoyed, but they shared many of his basic assumptions and perspectives. With hindsight, some have regretted that their dissertations were not brought together in a proper synthesis, for the unfortunate consequence was that broad questions concerning Sweden's policy were not addressed in depth, and the framework of small-state realism hampered an ethical or ideological discussion. Refugee policy, for example, was a field of research in the SUAV project, but the moral implications of Sweden's part in the destruction of European Jewry were never discussed, even though this was in accordance with the avowedly objective, non-normative ideals of the day. The Holocaust was hence not considered a part of Sweden's war history.[13]

There were some works, however, that tried to summarise the research and present a comprehensive picture. The historian Alf W. Johansson had written a SUAV dissertation, and in 1985 published an important study on the coalition government and foreign policy during the Second World War, centred on the wartime prime minister, Per Albin Hansson. Johansson described Swedish policy as one of negotiation rather than of concession, and his conclusions tended to confirm the small-state realism narrative. He characterised the foreign policy of the coalition government in a much-quoted phrase as the 'good management of fortunate circumstances.'[14]

A limited number of studies in the 1970s and 1980s took an alternative stance. Often they were not written by historians, but by specialists in literature, film and theatre. Yet, despite their focus on the intellectual and spiritual resistance to Nazism among the writers and artists, they helped to reinforce an impression fully in line with small-state realism: the Swedes had done what they could to keep the Nazis in check.[15] Openly critical studies of the political and cultural trends of the 1930s and 1940s were rare, and thanks to their rarity they would be regarded as exceptions to a general rule.[16] Things were to change, however.

Swedish Counter-Narratives

In spite of the power and dominance of the small-state realistic interpretation during the post-war era, a couple of distinct counter-narratives can be discerned. They occurred so sporadically between 1945 and 1990 that it is hard to talk of a continuous narration. Instead, they resembled what can be identified as counter-voices, divergent opinions which never managed to gain a public hearing. In terms of structure and form, however, they had much in common with the hegemonic small-state realistic narrative. In both, certain victims, heroes, enemies and scapegoats were at the heart of the interpretation. Moreover, the master narrative as well as the counter-narratives represented a particular set of core values, often expressed in a geographic orientation or ideological loyalty. Finally, a specific narrator can be recognised, that is, a person or a group that incarnated the narrative. All counter-narratives had a common denominator in their rejection of small-state realism, often as criticism of both Swedish policy during the war and national self-righteousness after 1945. Sweden was regularly portrayed as a petty country, unable to see the larger currents that shaped the time.

The *moral counter-narrative* was observable here and there during the post-war period. The leitmotiv of this critical interpretation was that the coalition government, with its concessions to Nazi Germany, had pursued a morally irresponsible policy, whose only purpose had been unconditionally to keep Sweden out of the great power conflict. The guiding star had been unscrupulous pragmatism. The wartime government was accused of being incapable of seeing the Second World War for what it really had been: a *moral* struggle between democracy and dictatorship, liberty and oppression, good and evil. On the contrary, leading Swedish politicians acted in a cowardly manner and were nationally narrow-minded, bargaining with the fundamental values of democracy. According to this narrative, the policy of concession only served to prolong the war and prevented the world from drawing attention to Nazi crimes. Of course, the other narratives of Sweden and the Second World War also contained certain ethical principles. This particular counter-narrative, however, was not primarily based on ideology or power politics but on moral values, which entailed a powerful moral appeal directed to the Swedish establishment.

An explicit, passionately anti-Nazi stance was at the core of the moral counter-narrative, visible not least in its defence of democracy, the rule of law and human dignity. In the moral staging, prominent wartime anti-Nazis such as Torgny Segerstedt, Eyvind Johnson and Amelie Posse-Brázdová were the leading actors, as were humanitarian heroes including Raoul Wallenberg and Folke Bernadotte. The scapegoats were the coalition government and the so-called *roddare* ('oarsmen'), those who swiftly changed sides at the end of the war.

Many of the leading wartime opponents of National Socialism did what they could to promulgate a moral counter-narrative in the early post-war years. Immediately after the end of the war, newspapers such as *Göteborgs Handels- och Sjöfarts-Tidning* and *Expressen* were its mouthpiece. In other newspapers, individual journalists and publicists embraced the narrative, among them Johannes Wickman, the foreign editor of the leading *Dagens Nyheter*, who had fiercely censured official Swedish policies during the war. In addition, a small number of Jewish intellectuals belonged to this group. Hugo Valentin, a historian and a writer, had already in October 1942 drawn public attention in Sweden to the ongoing Nazi mass murder in Continental Europe. He and other Jewish writers continued to cover the issue in journals such as *Judisk krönika* and *Judisk tidskrift* after 1945.[17]

A moral undercurrent was to be seen in isolated novels and television programmes from the late 1960s, from Per Olof Enquist's

Legionärerna ('The legionnaires') to Kenne Fant's book on the wartime foreign minister, Christian Günther. A more fiery debate was triggered by the American television production *Holocaust*, which was broadcast in Sweden in the spring of 1979. Some commentators asked whether this theme really concerned a Swedish audience, but a more moral narrative also broke through. The journalist Göran Rosenberg, for example, could not let a counter-narrative of Sweden and the Second World War pass unnoticed. In a series of articles in *Aftonbladet*, 'Sweden in the Shadow of the Holocaust', he shed light on Sweden's restrictive refugee policy towards persecuted Jews and the impact of anti-Semitism on Swedish society. In a larger perspective, however, the moral counter-narrative was weak and marginal. It was observable here and there during the whole post-war period, but it was only in the 1990s that it managed to challenge the small-state realistic interpretation.[18]

The *Communist counter-narrative* originated in a Marxist-Leninist interpretation of the Second World War. It shared many of its features with the moral counter-narrative, most fundamentally the indignation at the concessions to Nazi Germany and the failure to confront Sweden's 'brown' past after 1945. But the list of crimes did not end there. According to the Communist interpretation, Fascism had been an upper-class phenomenon, even though Germanophile attitudes infused large sectors of Swedish society from the royal family to police authorities, the army and high finance. The principal difference between the Communist and the moral counter-narratives was the programmatic anti-Fascism that underpinned the former. The Second World War was part of the greater class struggle, and National Socialism was simply regarded as an agent of aggressive German capitalism. The Communist heroes were either the radical resistance movement who had been fighting the Fascists or those who had joined the Red Army in its struggle. During the Cold War, this led its opponents to stress the great role the Soviet Union played in the outcome of the Second World War. Politicians, intellectuals and journalists with radical left-wing inclinations embraced the Communist counter-narrative.[19]

Unlike many other Western European countries, the Second World War did not play any major role in the Swedish radical movement of the late 1960s and early 1970s. Traces of a Communist counter-narrative could doubtless be found, but the war was never a driving force in Swedish debates or actions. To conclude, the Communist counter-narrative was transmitted in various left-wing circles throughout the post-war period, but it failed to have a significant impact on Swedish society as a whole.[20]

The most peripheral alternative interpretation of the Second World War was the *ultra-nationalist counter-narrative*. At the same time chauvinistically Swedish and pro-German, it combined ideals that did not find favour with the post-war public discourse. The ultra-nationalist narrative included a deep-seated identification with the desires and aspirations of Nazi Germany, an understanding that was sometimes transformed into a dream of the fulfilment of a Swedish–German alliance. Among its enemies were the hypocritical politicians and conceited moralists who had humiliated Sweden's national values, while the great national heroes included first and foremost King Gustaf V.

Ideologically, the ultra-nationalist counter-narrative rested upon anti-Communism, royalism and patriotism. After the war, it showed its loyalty to older Swedish and European traditions. In the war years, its supporters had belonged to Germanophile, right-wing circles (*Svenska nationella förbundet* and other similar societies), but the number of followers diminished drastically after 1945. In the post-war period, the ultra-nationalist counter-narrative kept itself to obscure milieus and peripheral journals; memoirs, diaries and letters; right-wing national newspapers and publications; and organisations that still embraced authoritarian nationalism and longed for the resurrection of temporarily defeated Germany. Biographically it was associated with men such as Rütger Essén, Einar Åberg and Carl Ernfrid Carlberg. In a wider public sphere, the ultra-nationalist interpretation was a counter-narrative in its most genuine sense, a terrible reminder of what had been overthrown.[21]

The small-state realistic narrative had taken possession of the collective Swedish memory of the Second World War, and the counter-narratives never managed to break through. The German historian Nicolas Berg has analysed how 'memory conflicts' (*Erinnerungskämpfe*) took place in the Federal Republic and how dominant opinions on the Third Reich were challenged. In Sweden, too, the master narrative was criticised and rejected in the post-war period, but far greater upheavals were needed to really challenge the small-state realistic interpretation and its position as a hegemonic narrative.[22]

The Moral Narrative

With the fall of the Berlin Wall and the collapse of the Soviet Union, an epoch reached its end. More than that, however, the traditions and objectives that had helped guide people and societies were called into question by the end of the Cold War. This has been called the 'crisis of the narratives'.[23]

In Sweden, the strong small-state realistic narrative mouldered in the course of the 1990s. In the preface to *Heder och samvete* (1991; 'Honour and Conscience'), a hugely influential book that marked the beginning of a new attitude toward Sweden during the Second World War, the author Maria-Pia Boëthius declared:

> This is a history book for those who were born after the war; an indictment, a list of sins and a contribution to the debate. The post-war generation in Sweden knows extraordinarily little about Sweden and the Second World War. This might be a part of our general lack of a sense of history, this might be a conspiracy of silence. Sweden's role during the Second World War was not glorious.[24]

Boëthius's polemic launched a series of controversies surrounding the small-state realistic narrative in the 1990s. Older reviewers tended to dismiss her book as a superficial pamphlet, but her younger readers were much more receptive. In that respect, *Heder och samvete* paved the way for a whole range of critical books and articles in the 1990s on everything from Nazi gold to Swedes who had fought Hitler.[25]

In spite of the symbolic importance of Boëthius's historical accusation, a prelude to the collective self-examination of the 1990s could already be heard in the late 1980s. Zarah Leander's career in the Third Reich, for example, was debated in the press in 1988. In the post-war period, the Swedish star had not been regarded as a political animal, but rather as a diva, a naïve and successful prima donna who had charmed audiences in Nazi Germany and elsewhere. By the end of the 1980s, however, a much more critical narrative prevailed, portraying Leander as a woman of doubtful reputation who had enjoyed the company of senior Nazis without hesitation.[26] At the same time, Ingmar Bergman's memoir *Laterna Magica* had elicited some public response after he had admitted his fascination with National Socialism in his youth. A few years later, a book on the Wallenbergs, an important financial dynasty, and their relationship with Nazi Germany also sparked a public debate.[27]

This change in mood must be seen against the backdrop of international developments in the late 1980s. For instance, the *Historikerstreit* in West Germany in 1986–1988 was thoroughly discussed in Sweden and may have prompted Swedish self-examination. Other national confrontations, including the controversies surrounding the Austrian president Kurt Waldheim, the philosopher Martin Heidegger, and the French Vichy regime, were also commented on in the media. All in all, these public European disputes in the late 1980s were the harbingers of the intensive struggle with the war legacy in the 1990s.

Although it is impossible to establish a specific date when the change took place, the years around 1990 marked the beginning of the gradual transition from a patriotic to a universalistic narrative of the Second World War in Sweden. In essence, the dominant national interpretation underwent the same transformation that the rest of Europe was experiencing. Self-righteousness gave way to self-criticism, national sovereignty to international commitment, and security to human dignity. The narrative became eminently moral once it revolved around the Holocaust.

In the 1990s, Swedish historiography on the Second World War shifted focus. An event of symbolic significance occurred in 1995, when Alf W. Johansson, one of the leading experts in the field, took the opportunity at a major conference held to mark the fiftieth anniversary of the end of the war to give a speech that was to have far-reaching implications. In his soul-searching address, Johansson described the view that had permeated the post-war interpretation of Sweden's conduct during the war, including the SUAV project:

> Sweden had been confronted with a ruthless and aggressive great power and had no choice but to give way. This had been a wise policy, because it had saved the peace. However, the ideological perspective on the war had to be pushed aside if this line was to be consistently argued, and this created a strange duality in the Swedish consciousness.[28]

It was precisely this perspective that was the target of the moral criticism of the 1990s. Small-state realism had had the effect of excluding important aspects of the Second World War from the analysis. Historians had unquestioningly adopted the coalition government's perspective as their own, neglecting to raise the moral issues. In his self-critical speech, Johansson discussed Wilhelm M. Carlgren's comprehensive account from 1973 and his own book from the mid 1980s. Both, in his opinion, were firmly within 'the framework of the same paradigm, namely small-state realism, and in that sense were a defence of wartime policy'.[29]

Alf W. Johansson's reconsideration was not an isolated phenomenon. On the contrary, in the late 1990s and early 2000s a whole range of new studies on anti-Semitism, racial biology, the Holocaust and Swedish relations with Nazi Germany were published. The majority were written by a younger generation of researchers, most of them born in the 1960s, including Lars M. Andersson, Lena Berggren, Heléne Lööw and Mattias Tydén. Their critical approach to the moral issues distinguished them from the older historians in the SUAV project, who had been born in the 1930s or 1940s.[30]

In 2000, the Swedish Research Council launched a major new research project, 'Sveriges förhållande till nazismen, Nazityskland och Förintelsen' (SweNaz; 'Sweden's Relations with Nazism, Nazi Germany and the Holocaust'). It drew scholars from across the humanities and social sciences. In contrast to the SUAV project of the 1970s, SweNaz specifically took the Holocaust as its departure point.[31] Sweden and the Holocaust had first been treated in a historical analysis in 1987 by an American historian, Steven Koblik. Another American historian, Paul A. Levine, living in Sweden, wrote the second monograph on the theme.[32] From the late 1990s, however, Swedish historians not only began to publish on the subject, but scholars from many other disciplines also made important contributions to the history of Sweden and the Holocaust.[33]

As an official confirmation of the general acceptance of the new moral narrative, Prime Minister Göran Persson launched the project 'Levande historia' ('Living History') in 1997, to promote democracy, tolerance and human rights, with the Holocaust as the point of departure. The Stockholm International Forum on the Holocaust in 2000 was a decisive moment for this new universalistic narrative.[34]

The Crisis of Consensus

In a broader international perspective, certain peculiarities in Sweden's confronting of the patriotic interpretation stand out. The criticism of the small-state realistic framework coincided with, and partly overlapped, a more general criticism of the groundwork of post-war society. With a series of debates on instrumental rationality, eugenic sterilisations and disrespect for individual freedom, the field opened on Swedish welfare state. The policy of neutrality and non-alignment, cornerstones of Swedish foreign policy during the Cold War, was portrayed as an exercise in hypocrisy. In general, the 1990s can be regarded as 'the decade of debates,' as a time when the whole post-war construction was challenged and discussed.[35]

Not by coincidence, Sweden's confrontations with the small-state realistic narrative ran parallel to a more general examination of post-war society. In Sweden as in other parts of Europe, the patriotic interpretation of the Second World War had since 1945 lived symbiotically with broader post-war narratives. The strength of the Swedish interpretation can be explained by the fact that it formed a solid basis for the welfare state in the Cold War era. It efficiently underpinned an idea of Sweden as a neutral, democratic and flourishing country, where everybody worked for the benefit of the common good and where peaceful conflict solutions were preferred. Furthermore, the small-state realistic understanding merged with the hegemonic master narrative of modern Sweden adhered to by the Social Democrats and the majority of the centre-right opposition in the post-war period. Even though this narrative of democracy, welfare and rationalism was challenged from the 1960s on (by, in turn, the New Left, the women's movement, the Green movement and new liberal currents), Sweden and the Second World War was never a prime target for their attacks. Small-state realism could remain an important part in Sweden's self-understanding even when the master narrative was called into question.[36]

Nevertheless, it is misleading to interpret the small-state realistic interpretation as 'a conspiracy of silence,' as a cunning form of manipulation by a malignant government. The patriotic narrative had its roots in questions of identity and historical understanding, but also in the conclusions drawn from Sweden's experience of the Second World War in the late 1940s and early 1950s. Equally, the transformation of the patriotic narrative into a universalistic story in the 1990s was facilitated by the universalistic tenor of the patriotic Swedish interpretation. In the heyday of small-state realism, after all, it could easily be amalgamated with a kind of small-state idealism. With its progressive character, which underscored universal values such as international solidarity, civil rights and general welfare, much of its import remained intact even when the structure had changed. To put it differently, the lesson of small-state realism remained even when small-state realism itself was discredited.

The consensual crisis paved the way for a new kind of consensus. The moral narrative that emerged in the early 1990s became more and more hegemonic. These changes reflect a general European development, but it is nevertheless important to take the specific Swedish characteristics into consideration, for new universalistic narrative was not just a historical interpretation; as always, historical narratives have at least as much to do with the present and the future as with the past. Some commentators, including the historian Klas-Göran Karlsson, have seen this development in the light of various Europeanisation processes in Sweden in the 1990s. To be a genuine part of the wider European project (Sweden became a member of the European Union in 1995), the country 'also had to come to terms – albeit belatedly – with the unifying experience of war and its symbolism.' A new approach to the history of Sweden during the war was therefore called for.[37]

Toward Pluralism?

In 2005, sixty years after the end of the Second World War, the Swedish Prime Minister Göran Persson took part in several commemorative ceremonies. Unexpectedly, he chose to defend Sweden's actions during the war. For instance, on Victory Day, 9 May, he visited Moscow. He declared that if more European nations had been as peaceful as Sweden, the world would have been a better place to live in. In subsequent interviews, the Prime Minister added that he did not see any reason for Swedes to apologise for their neutrality during the war. On several other occasions, moreover, he stressed the need for a continued appreciation of Swedish wartime heroes, including Raoul Wallenberg and Folke Bernadotte.[38]

Göran Persson had been instrumental in the launching of the Living History project in the late 1990s, and he had also been one of the key figures at the Stockholm International Forum on the Holocaust in 2000. In 2005, however, he seems to have abandoned this more self-critical stance and rediscovered small-state realism. Some commentators interpreted his swing in the light of current Swedish politics: when support for both the Social Democratic Party and the European project were on the decline, Göran Persson sought to reinvigorate an older and more patriotic Swedish narrative based on modernity and neutrality.[39]

Although a political interpretation of Göran Persson's statements might be fruitful, there are signs that the overall narrative of Sweden and the Second World War has shifted in the course of the 2000s. It would be an exaggeration to say that the war is no longer controversial or that the understanding of the war has been transformed in accordance with a Hegelian scheme, where the thesis (the small-state realistic narrative) is replaced by the antithesis (the moral narrative) which, finally, makes way for the synthesis. Rather, one might talk about a new pluralism, at least in the scholarly community.[40]

In 2007, for instance, the historians Lars M. Andersson and Mattias Tydén edited an anthology of eighteen articles, written by many of the researchers and journalists who had been engaged in the historical and public debate in the 1990s and 2000s on Sweden and Nazi Germany. The book gives examples of themes in today's historiography on Sweden during the Second World War, but also of the scope of the various interpretations. In one of the sections, for example, three well-established historians, Klas Åmark, Sverker Oredsson and Kent Zetterberg, give three different judgements on the Swedish policy of neutrality during the war.[41]

This is not the only sign of a growing pluralism in recent years. The SweNaz project has several offshoots, for example Henrik Bachner's book about anti-Semitism in inter-war, intellectual circles and Mats Deland's examination of Baltic war criminals who found a sanctuary in post-war Sweden. Despite their differences, these studies share a common critical stance and a willingness to treat neglected or morally sensitive subjects.[42] At the same time, the first comprehensive overview of Sweden during the Second World War for English-speaking readers was published in 2010, in which John Gilmour, an Honorary Fellow in Scandinavian Studies at the University of Edinburgh, draws on both older and newer historical research. He regrets that the 'interest in Sweden's war has moved towards simpler polemical issues'. Although he discusses questions of race and refugee policy critically, his general conclusions by and large adhere more to a small-state realistic paradigm than a moral one.[43]

It is too early to conclude that the moral narrative was a parenthesis in Swedish historiography and public memory. But what we are seeing now is probably the end of its heyday. In the future, the moral perspective may be just one of many. What is clear is that the Second World War continues to be political, moral and existential dynamite, in Sweden and elsewhere.[44]

Notes

1 This article enlarges on Johan Östling, 'Swedish Narratives of the Second World War: A European Perspective', *Contemporary European History*, 17, 2008a:2; and Johan Östling, *Nazismens sensmoral: Svenska erfarenheter i andra världskrigets efterdyning* (Stockholm, 2008b).

2 Excellent bibliographical works on Sweden and the Second World War include Stig Ekman & Klas Åmark (eds.), *Sweden's Relations with Nazism, Nazi Germany and the Holocaust: A Survey of Research* (Stockholm, 2003); and Patrick

Vonderau, *Schweden und das nationalsozialistische Deutschland: Eine annotierte Bibliographie der deutschsprachigen Forschungsliteratur: 825 Einträge – 439 Annotationen* (Stockholm, 2003).

3 Östling 2008b, 103–112.

4 Alf W. Johansson, 'Neutrality and Modernity: The Second World War and Sweden's National Identity', in: Stig Ekman & Nils Edling (eds.), *War Experience, Self Image and National Identity: The Second World War as Myth and History* (Stockholm, 1997), 176. See also Max Liljefors & Ulf Zander, 'Det neutrala landet Ingenstans: Bilder av andra världskriget och den svenska utopin', *Scandia*, 69, 2003:2; and Claus Bryld, '"The Five Accursed Years": Danish Perception and Usage of the Period of the German Occupation, With a Wider View to Norway and Sweden', *Scandinavian Journal of History*, 32, 2007:1.

5 Quoted in Alf W. Johansson, *Den nazistiska utmaningen: Aspekter på andra* världskriget (Stockholm, 2006), 277.

6 Johansson 2006, 280–287; Bo Stråth, *Folkhemmet mot Europa: Ett historiskt perspektiv på 90-talet* (Stockholm, 1993). See also Alf W. Johansson, 'Inledning: Svensk nationalism och identitet efter andra världskriget', in: Alf W. Johansson (ed.), *Vad är Sverige?: Röster om svensk nationell identitet* (Stockholm, 2001).

7 Jeffrey C. Alexander, 'On the Social Construction of Moral Universals: The "Holocaust" from War Crime to Trauma Drama', in: Jeffrey C. Alexander et al. (eds.), *Cultural Trauma and Collective Identity* (Berkeley, 2004), 209.

8 See, for example, Ulf Zander, '*Holocaust* at the Limits: Historical Culture and the Nazi Genocide in the Television Era', in: Klas-Göran Karlsson & Ulf Zander (eds.), *Echoes of the Holocaust: Historical Cultures in Contemporary Europe* (Lund, 2003); and Max Liljefors & Ulf Zander, 'Der Zweite Weltkrieg und die schwedische Utopie', in: Monika Flacke (ed.), *Mythen der Nationen: 1945 – Arena der Erinnerungen*, 2 vols. (Berlin, 2004).

9 Östling 2008b, 63–91.

10 Gunnar Hägglöf, *Svensk krigshandelspolitik under andra världskriget* (Stockholm, 1958); Åke Thulstrup, *Med lock och pock: Tyska försök att påverka svensk opinion 1933–45* (Stockholm, 1962). See also Stig Ekman, 'Introduction', in: Stig Ekman & Klas Åmark (eds.), *Sweden's Relations with Nazism, Nazi Germany and the Holocaust: A Survey of Research* (Stockholm, 2003), 16–22.

11 Ekman 2003, 20–27; Johansson 2006, 284–285.

12 Wilhelm M. Carlgren, *Svensk utrikespolitik 1939–1945* (Stockholm, 1973). An abridged English edition was published a few years later as Wilhelm M. Carlgren, *Swedish Foreign Policy during the Second World War* (London, 1977).

13 Ekman 2003, 22–30; Johansson 2006, 284–285.

14 Alf W. Johansson, *Per Albin och kriget: Samlingsregeringen och utrikespolitiken under andra världskriget* (Stockholm, 1985), 416. See also Stig Ekman (ed.), *Stormaktstryck och småstatspolitik: Aspekter på svensk politik under andra världskriget* (Stockholm, 1986).

15 Bengt Landgren, *Hjalmar Gullberg och beredskapslitteraturen: Studier i svensk dikt och politisk debatt 1933–1942* (Stockholm, 1975); Martin Lind, *Kristendom och nazism: Frågan om kristendom och nazism belyst av olika ställningstaganden i*

Tyskland och Sverige 1933–1945 (Lund, 1975); Louise Drangel, *Den kämpande demokratin: En studie i antinazistisk opinionsrörelse 1935–1945* (Stockholm, 1976); Willmar Sauter, *Theater als Widerstand: Wirkung und Wirkungsweise eines politischen Theaters: Faschismus und Judendarstellung auf der schwedischen Bühne 1936–1941* (Stockholm, 1979).

16 Tomas Forser, *Bööks 30-tal: En studie i ideologi* (Stockholm, 1976); Jan Olsson, *Svensk spelfilm under andra världskriget* (Lund, 1979).

17 Karin Sjögren, *Judar i det svenska folkhemmet: Minne och identitet i Judisk krönika 1948–1958* (Eslöv, 2001), 141–143.

18 Zander 2003. One example of a moral narrative in a scholarly work is Radko Kejzlar, *Literatur und Neutralität: Zur schwedischen Literatur der Kriegs- und Nachkriegszeit* (Basel, 1984).

19 Erik Blomberg, *Demokratin och kriget* (Stockholm, 1945); Hilding Hagberg, *Röd bok om svart tid* (Staffanstorp, 1966).

20 See, however, Wolfgang Butt, *Mobilmachung des Elfenbeinturms: Reaktionen auf den Faschismus in der schwedischen Literatur 1933–1939* (Neumünster, 1977) for a German example.

21 Heléne Lööw, *Nazismen i Sverige 1924–1979: Pionjärerna, partierna, propagandan* (Stockholm, 2004); Stéphane Bruchfeld, 'Grusade drömmar: Svenska "nationella" och det tyska nederlaget 1945', in: Charlotta Brylla, Birgitta Almgren & Frank-Michael Kirsch (eds.), *Bilder i kontrast: Interkulturella processer Sverige/Tyskland i skuggan av nazismen 1933–1945* (Aalborg, 2005).

22 Nicolas Berg, *Der Holocaust und die westdeutschen Historiker: Erforschung und Erinnerung* (Göttingen, 2003).

23 Kim Salomon, Lisbeth Larsson & Håkan Arvidsson (eds.), *Hotad idyll: Berättelser om svenskt folkhem och kallt krig* (Lund, 2004), 7–17.

24 'Detta är en historiebok för efterkrigsfödda; en anklagelseakt, ett syndaregister och en debattbok. Efterkrigsgenerationerna i Sverige vet synnerligen lite om Sverige och andra världskriget. Det kan vara en del av vår allmänna historielöshet, det kan vara en tystnadens konspiration. Sveriges roll under andra världskriget var inte ärofull.' See Maria-Pia Boëthius, *Heder och samvete: Sverige och andra världskriget* (Stockholm, 1991), 9.

25 Ulf Zander, *Fornstora dagar, moderna tider: Bruk av och debatter om svensk historia från sekelskifte till sekelskifte* (Lund, 2001), 445–455.

26 Östling 2008b, 284–286.

27 Ingmar Bergman, *Laterna Magica* (Stockholm, 1987); Gerard Aalders & Cees Wiebes, *Affärer till varje pris: Wallenbergs hemliga stöd till nazisterna* (Stockholm, 1989).

28 Johansson 1997, 176.

29 Johansson 1997, 181.

30 Sverker Oredsson, *Lunds universitet under andra världskriget: Motsättningar, debatter och hjälpinsatser* (Lund, 1996); Gunnar Richardson, *Beundran och fruktan: Sverige inför Tyskland 1940–1942* (Stockholm, 1996); Lena Berggren, *Nationell upplysning: Drag i den svenska antisemitismens idéhistoria* (Stockholm, 1999); Henrik Bachner, *Återkomsten: Antisemitism i Sverige efter 1945*

(Stockholm, 1999); Lars M. Andersson, *En jude är en jude är en jude …: Representationer av 'juden' i svensk skämtpress omkring 1900–1930* (Lund, 2000); Henrik Carlsson, *Medborgarskap och diskriminering: Östjudar och andra invandrare i Sverige 1860–1920* (Uppsala, 2004); Heléne Lööw, *Nazismen i Sverige 1924–1979: Pionjärerna, partierna, propagandan* (Stockholm, 2004); Ingrid Lomfors, *Blind fläck: Minne och glömska kring svenska Röda korsets hjälpinsats i Nazityskland 1945* (Stockholm, 2005); Håkan Blomqvist, *Nation, ras och civilisation i svensk arbetarrörelse före nazismen* (Stockholm, 2006); Henrik Rosengren, *'Judarnas Wagner': Moses Pergament och den kulturella identifikationens dilemma omkring 1920–1950* (Lund, 2007); Mikael Byström, *En broder, gäst och parasit: Uppfattningar och föreställningar om utlänningar, flyktingar och flyktingpolitik i svensk offentlig debatt 1942–1947* (Stockholm, 2006); Karin Kvist Geverts, *Ett främmande element i nationen: Svensk flyktingpolitik och de judiska flyktingarna 1938–1944* (Uppsala, 2008). See also Ingvar Svanberg & Mattias Tydén (eds.), *Sverige och Förintelsen: Debatt och dokument om Europas judar 1933–1945* (Stockholm, 1997); Håkan Blomqvist, *Gåtan Nils Flyg och nazismen* (Stockholm, 1999); Håkan Blomqvist, *Socialdemokrat och antisemit?: Den dolda historien om Arthur Engberg* (Stockholm, 2001); Göran Blomberg, *Mota Moses i grind: Ariseringsiver och antisemitism i Sverige 1933–1943* (Stockholm, 2003); Henrik Karlsson, *Det fruktade märket: Wilhelm Peterson-Berger, antisemitismen och antinazismen* (Malmö, 2005); and Lars M. Andersson & Karin Kvist Gevers (eds.), *En problematisk relation? Flyktingpolitik och judiska flyktingar i Sverige 1920–1950* (Uppsala, 2008). Of course, not all of them belonged to the younger generation; Gunnar Richardson was born in 1924 and Sverker Oredsson in 1937.

31 'Forskningsprogrammet "Sveriges förhållande till nazismen, Nazityskland och Förintelsen"', <http://www.vr.se/download/18.bfcea3310ab2bd97898000214/Nazismen.pdf> accessed on 1 December 2010.

32 Steven Koblik, *'Om vi teg, skulle stenarna ropa': Sverige och judeproblemet 1933–1945* (Stockholm, 1987); Levine 1996.

33 Birgitta Almgren, *Illusion und Wirklichkeit: Individuelle und kollektive Denkmuster in nationalsozialistischer Kulturpolitik und Germanistik in Schweden 1928–1945* (Stockholm, 2001); Max Liljefors, *Bilder av Förintelsen: Mening, minne, kompromettering* (Lund, 2002); Anders Ohlsson, *'Men ändå måste jag berätta': Studier i skandinavisk förintelselitteratur* (Nora, 2002); Birgitta Almgren, *Drömmen om Norden: Nazistisk infiltration i Sverige 1933–1945* (Stockholm, 2005); Charlotta Brylla, Birgitta Almgren & Frank-Michael Kirsch (eds.), *Bilder i kontrast: Interkulturella processer Sverige/Tyskland i skuggan av nazismen 1933–1945* (Aalborg, 2005); Greger Andersson & Ursula Geisler (eds.), *Fruktan, fascination och frändskap: Det svenska musiklivet och nazismen* (Malmö, 2006); Anders Jarlert, *Judisk 'ras' som äktenskapshinder i Sverige: Effekten av Nürnberglagarna i Svenska kyrkans statliga funktion som lysningsförrättare 1935–1945* (Malmö, 2006); Petra Garberding, *Musik och politik i skuggan av nazismen: Kurt Atterberg och de svensk-tyska musikrelationerna* (Lund, 2007); Birgit Karlsson, *Egenintresse eller samhällsintresse: Nazityskland och svensk skogsindustri*

1933–1945 (Lund, 2007); Martin Fritz, *Sveriges tyskgruvor: Tyskägda gruvor i Sverige under andra världskriget* (Lund, 2007).

34 David Ludvigsson, '"Levande historia" – inte bara levande historia', in: Carsten Tage Nielsen, Dorthe Gert Simonsen & Lene Wul (eds.), *Rapporter til Det 24. Nordiske Historikermøde, Århus 9.–13. august 2001: Mod nye historier* (Århus, 2001); Klas-Göran Karlsson, 'The Holocaust as Politics and Use of History – the Example of Living History', in: Kurt Almqvist & Kay Glans (eds.), *The Swedish Success Story?* (Stockholm, 2004).

35 Zander 2001, 402–459; Åsa Linderborg, *Socialdemokraterna skriver historia: Historieskrivning som ideologisk maktresurs 1892–2000* (Stockholm, 2001), 419–423; Göran Rosenberg, 'The Crisis of Consensus in Postwar Sweden', in: Nina Witoszek & Lars Trägårdh (eds.), *Culture and Crisis: The Case of Germany and Sweden* (New York, 2002).

36 Martin Wiklund, *I det modernas landskap: Historisk orientering och kritiska berättelser om det moderna Sverige mellan 1960 och 1990* (Eslöv, 2006).

37 Karlsson 2004, 245.

38 Ulf Zander, 'To Rescue or be Rescued: The Liberation of Bergen-Belsen and the White Buses in British and Swedish Historical Cultures', in: Klas-Göran Karlsson & Ulf Zander (eds.), *The Holocaust on Post-War Battlefields: Genocide as Historical Culture* (Malmö, 2006), 372–373.

39 Per T. Ohlsson, 'När Persson flammar stolt', *Sydsvenska Dagbladet Snällposten*, 26 June 2005.

40 Of course, the moral narrative had been challenged before. For a critical view, see, for example, Kent Zetterberg, 'Det neutrala Sveriges skuld och ansvar: Till frågan om den svenska politiken under det andra världskriget och den svenska debatten efter kriget', in: Kent Zetterberg & Gunnar Åselius (eds.), *Historia, krig och statskonst: En vänbok till Klaus-Richard Böhme* (Stockholm, 2000).

41 Lars M Andersson & Mattias Tydén (eds.), *Sverige och Nazityskland: Skuldfrågor och moraldebatt* (Stockholm, 2007).

42 Henrik Bachner, *'Judefrågan': Debatt om antisemitism i 1930-talets Sverige* (Stockholm, 2009); Mats Deland, *Purgatorium: Sverige och andra världskrigets förbrytare* (Stockholm, 2010). A further example is Paul A. Levine, *Raoul Wallenberg in Budapest: Myth, History and Holocaust* (Edgware, 2010). Klas Åmark, *Att bo granne med ondskan* (forthcoming 2011) will synthesise the research on Sweden's relations with Nazi Germany.

43 John Gilmour, *Sweden, the Swastika and Stalin: The Swedish Experience in the Second World War* (Edinburgh, 2010), 234 and 281–287.

44 A recent example is the debate sparked by two books published by the journalist Henrik Arnstad, *Spelaren Christian Günther: Sverige under andra världskriget* (Stockholm, 2006) and *Skyldig till skuld: En europeisk resa i Nazitysklands skugga* (Stockholm, 2009). His accounts accord with the moral narrative of the war and have been contested both by Swedish and Finnish historians. See, for example, Henrik Meinander, 'Arnstads bok är inte seriös', *Svenska*

Dagbladet, 3 December 2006; and Mats Bergquist, 'Revisionismens lockelser: Debatten om Sverige under andra världskriget', in: Mats Bergquist & Alf W. Johansson (eds.), *Säkerhetspolitik och historia: Essäer om stormaktspolitiken och Norden under sjuttio år* (Stockholm, 2007).

CHAPTER 7

Nordic Foundation Myths after 1945

A European Context

Bo Stråth

The 'Hour Zero' Myths of 1945 and 1989

The world of yesterday, it now seems, collapsed in 1989–1991 with the end of the Cold War. The world of the day before yesterday collapsed first in 1914 and then again in 1939. Old points of orientation in time and space ceased to function. This is what 1914, 1939 and 1989 have in common. In order better to understand the dramatic upheavals around 1990, a search began for new heuristic points of departure, as it had done after 1914 and 1939.

The year 1989 was constructed as a new 'hour zero'. Its predecessor was 1945. The East–West divide of the Cold War was to be bridged by the project of a unified Europe. While the myth of the Hour Zero in 1945 had drawn on the heroism of the resistance movements, this once hegemonic master narrative now receded into a foggy past, challenged by new histories. The previous emphasis on resistance shifted to reflections on the Second World War that emphasised collaboration.

The shift often occurred as a consequence of political appeals for a new history and a new truth. These claims had a moralistic subtext. A new future required new values. Truth became a key word, old truths were renamed hypocrisy. History commissions were established in several countries to investigate and reconsider the past. With the straitjacket of the Cold War no longer a factor, all over Europe there was obvious political interest in rethinking the past.[1] The shift was far from being an exclusive, academic issue confined to professional historians.

Across the world, 1990 was imagined as a temporal divide between before and after the collapse of the Soviet empire. The collapse inspired new imaginings of the future, which, in turn, required the outline of a new past. The end of the Cold War led to a renegotiation of the histories of the European nation-states. Until then, the histories and foundation myths had risen from the previous divide of a similar magnitude, the Second World War. The important question here is *how* the narratives changed.

One way to understand the shift is the end-of-history (Fukuyama) and final-victory-of-liberalism rhetoric that emerged after the Soviet collapse.[2] A new future under the motto of liberalism, human rights and universalism required a new design for the past. The historical moment of the fall of the Wall provided politics with a moralistic dimension. The Promised Land ahead demanded the squaring of past accounts. The *Realpolitiker* of the Cold War, with their auto-suggested foundation myths about heroic resistance against Nazism, were condemned. Collaboration replaced resistance as the label for the past.

Another crucial question is how strong the shift in views on the past in response to the events of 1989–1991 really was. To what extent had the post-1945 foundation myths been challenged or begun to erode before the end of the Cold War? The question is crucial to the Nordic cases, and is best tackled by looking first at the German case.

The German foundation myth after 1945 was based on the myth of the *Stunde Null*: everything started from scratch on the road toward the implementation of a Western-type democracy in post-war Germany. In most other countries, the foundation myths outlined their people as heroic resisters of the Nazi occupation. For them, too, 1945 emerged as an Hour Zero of sorts. The foundation myth was violently challenged in Germany by the generation of 1968, in search of clarification about what their fathers had done during the war. The children argued that there was considerable continuity between before and after 1945 among the economic and political elites as well as among civil servants and the military.

An important question is to what extent the other European foundation myths, built around the concept of resistance, were challenged, as the German *Stunde Null* had been, by the generations *before* 1990. *After* 1990, the identity-shaping narratives based on the memories of the Second World War and on experience of the Cold War were questioned everywhere. Heroic resistance histories were replaced by new narratives about less heroic collaboration with the Nazi occupiers. The developments in the Nordic countries analysed in this volume are in this respect part of a broader European pattern. And even though the Nordic confrontations were less prominent than '1968' in Germany, to what extent was the collapse of the narratives of resistance around 1990 foreboded by earlier critiques?

There are links between the situation around 1990 and the circumstances of 1945. Both years represent historical moments with Hour Zero feelings of a looming new world about to bury the old. However, critical historical research has subsequently found that there was much more continuity between the pre- and post-war worlds than the Hour Zero narrative admits. The question now, almost a generation after 1990, is how much of this is also true for the moment of the fall of the Wall. How valid is the watershed thesis of 1990? Was the collapse of the resistance narratives an immediate consequence of the implosion of the Soviet empire? When and how did the critique of the narratives launched after1945 really begin?

From History to Memory

The more general problem underpinning such questions is the conditions under which different views of history emerge when 'community' is constructed by processes of demarcation between Us and the Other, Now and Then. How are these views, these foundation myths, transformed, and what is the role of historians, the media, politicians, artists, architects, writers, film producers and so on? Professional historians are one group among several to participate in these processes. They do it in their own particular way, adhering to certain rules and methodologies, but we cannot consider them to have a privileged position, whereby others develop myths that are analysed by critical historians, who then tell the 'truth'. The problem of the construction of different narratives of the past is linked to the general issue of how community is constructed in the *Spannungsfeld* between images of the past and visions of the future, and how history has been interpreted and mediated in various settings. This, then, raises the question of why symbols and myths so often emerge in the framework of the nation and become *geschichtsmässig*, carriers of history.[3] *Geschichtsmässig* refers to such events and facts that make up historical narratives, and are the result of selections by historians and others grappling with memory politics.

In the wake of a more general acceptance of the 'postmodern' perspective developed by Hayden White, François Lyotard, Paul Ricœur, Jacques Derrida and Michel Foucault, the distinction between history, memory and myth has been blurred, and these categories are now seen as overlapping and supplementary.[4] However, against this backdrop of blurred distinctions there remains the question of why there has nevertheless been an obvious conceptual slide from history toward memory.

What are the origins of the notable career of the word 'memory' in historiographical discourse? Is the use of this word necessary and irreplaceable in today's historiography? When collective memory emerged in the 1980s as a subject of scholarly interest, it was imagined as a historical counter-concept, and as a critique of history's totalising aspects. Since this linguistic turn, however, the understanding of history itself has also changed, and there is a growing awareness of the rhetorical and linguistic limits of history writing.

The German Case

'Anti-Fascism' can be seen as an example – although an extreme one – of how myths become *geschichtsmässig*, capable of communicating key dimensions in constructions of collective memory.[5] Just as anti-Fascism was 'moulded' to produce a clear definition of 'democracy' in Western Europe, anti-Fascism became in the German 'Democratic' Republic the pivot of an ideology that defined 'democratic' in a remarkable way. Many German Communists had made sacrifices in their fight against the Nazi regime, and in this respect the emergence of anti-Fascism as a *raison d'être* of the GDR is understandable. However, very soon after 1945, the idea of anti-Fascism became fixed in distorted forms. For instance, it was anti-Fascism which motivated and justified the erection of the Berlin Wall in 1961.[6] In the 1980s, Luther, Frederick the Great and Bismarck were all taken on board by the regime and merged with anti-Fascism as elements in the historical justification of the GDR. Anti-Fascism and resistance against Nazism became early concepts in the Cold War struggle between East and West over the definition of democracy. This is why the terms had such punch.

However, a history where the Western Federal Republic comes out looking like a hero while the GDR is nothing more than a propaganda construction would be too simple. In the West, as Bernhard Giesen has shown, the combination of memory and oblivion after the war played down the Nazi past. This was a memory strategy that was not only supported by the Allied powers after the war, but was actually initiated by them in order to prevent a repetition of the desire for revenge provoked by the Treaty of Versailles. This strategy formed an important part of the framework of mental mobilisation during the Cold War that assigned guilt to the Nazi leaders for having seduced the German people who, in turn, were seen as being separate from the regime. Only with the Eichmann trial and the youth revolt in the 1960s ('1968') did ideas of collective guilt emerge in which Nazi terror was not confined to a ruling elite, but interpreted in terms of a broader and, at the same time, more specifically German history, the *Sonderweg*.[7]

That *Sieg Heil* salutes can once more be heard in the former GDR cannot, of course, be attributed to a single 'cause', but must be seen in the framework of a complex mythology. One element of this framework was the antagonistic and permanent dichotomy that developed between Communism and Nazism. When Communism collapsed, radical adversaries of the state could tap into the interaction between memory and oblivion and turn it in new directions by means of old symbols. Victor Klemperer, whose diaries span the 1940s and 1950s in the GDR, emphasised the continuity in language between Nazism and Communism. In July 1945, we find him asking whether there is any difference between Hitler's creation of language and truth and Stalin's. 'Every day I observe the continuity from the Third Reich's *Lingua Tertii Imperii* to the *Lingua Quartii Imperii* in the Soviet sphere', he wrote in October that year.[8] The use of neo-Nazi language after 1990 thus indicates that the continuity is still working. Klemperer's statement is remarkable given the role of anti-Fascism as the key concept in the legitimisation of the GDR regime.

Anti-Fascism meant that the Federal Republic was referred to as the heir of the Nazi regime. It was in Adenauer's Federal Republic that Klemperer saw the greatest evil despite the similarities between the Nazi and the Communist languages. There he perceived the forces that had made Hitler's dictatorship possible were still at work. From this perspective, the GDR was, despite all its faults, the more human alternative. This example shows that myths and collective identities, while they may appear to offer a clear demarcation between Us and Them, Now and Then, contain both contradictions and overlaps.

The German case does not deal with a foundation myth born in 1945 and extinguished in 1990. The case is much more complex, with a weave of continuities and discontinuities, divides and overlaps, not only between the Western and Eastern parts before 1990 but also within the West. The FRG represents a case of continuous challenges and new formulations of the identity-shaping outlines of the past.

The post-1945 *Stunde Null* myth about a gang of Nazi criminals seducing a whole nation was, as mentioned, challenged in the 1960s by a new generation. An early indication of a new perspective was Fritz Fisher's *Griff nach der Weltmacht* in 1961, which critically interpreted German imperialism as an important factor behind the outbreak of the First World War. His long-term view on the following world war also put 1933 in its historical context.[9] The generational revolt of 1968 left *Stunde Null* under massive attack for it had been produced in Nuremberg amid general social polarisation and radicalised political language. To attack the foundation myth was just one goal among many in a broader, radical, political programme. Historians followed suit, arguing for a new kind of history, with a focus on the social dimension of the past and on the sufferings of the lower classes, in accordance with social scientific theories. In the 1970s, it was the turn of the social historians, the *Gesellschaftshistoriker*, to debate how and when things went wrong in Germany. Was it in *Vormärz*, which ended in the abortive revolution of 1848? Or was it with the proclamation of the *Kaiserreich* in 1871? Or could Weimar have developed differently? The debate wove a narrative about a German *Sonderweg*, a separate trajectory in the Western course toward democracy, liberalism and welfare. German singularity was epitomised by a lack of liberalism in the wake of certain aristocratic and feudal structures. The issue at stake was when exactly this lack had become evident in European terms.

Such historical revisionism from the Left gained an ever greater acceptance in the self-understanding of the population in the 1970s and 1980s. The *Stunde Null* myth lost credibility. However, soon after the *Sonderweg* thesis had won a hegemonic position in the debate, it was conjured up from the right by Ernst Nolte and other conservative historians who argued that instead of representing a unique trajectory, Germany was comparable with the Soviet Union. The two totalitarian orders were much more entangled than had so far been admitted. National Socialism was a response to Bolshevism and Hitler a consequence of Lenin. Nolte challenged the argument of left wing historians that nothing, absolutely nothing, could be compared to Nazi crimes, of which the Holocaust was the lowest point. Nolte *did* compare the Holocaust and the Gulag.[10] His attack triggered the German *Historikerstreit*, where the social historians Hans-Ulrich Wehler and Jürgen Kocka, supported by the philosopher Jürgen Habermas, emerged as the advocates of the *Sonderweg* thesis.[11]

Since 1990, it has become commonplace to compare the Holocaust and the Gulag. The events in 1989–1991 played into the hands of Nolte and his supporters. The collapse of the Communist regimes, and the opening of their archives led to the unmasking of a pathologic system and its cruelties in rich detail. Once the perversities of Communism were at the forefront of social debate, the historians' reminders of the crimes of the Nazis receded. Ironically, historians on the Left also contributed to this shift of perspective. Jürgen Kocka's major international *Bürgertum* project at the University of Bielefeld in 1987–1988, which assembled historians and social scientists from both sides of the Atlantic and from Eastern and Western Europe, found nothing but *Sonderwege* in the plural all over Europe, and no single standard, although at the outset the normative underpinning of the project presumably was to confirm German singularity through a broad comparative approach. The unforeseen consequence was that Germany's fateful history was relativised.[12] The exceptional case came to be the norm, one among many. There was no standard European or Western development toward democracy and welfare, against which an exceptional case of deviation to set. The rejection of the *Sonderweg* thesis meant the shift toward the language of European diversity.

The next narrative shift of emphasis came a decade later in the 2000s, when growing attention was paid to the German victims of the Second World War, be they women and old people on the home front or the hundreds of thousands killed in the Allied air raids. The war was not only a matter of German victimisers but also of German victims. A book that attracted much attention was Günther Grass' fictionalised account of the torpedoing of a German refugee ship in the Baltic at the end of the war.[13]

This outline of the German memory construction from 1945 until the 1990s shows a narrative that is complex and full of contradictions as well as overlap, discontinuity as well as continuity. The argument is that rather than a *Sonderweg*, Germany in this respect represents a model. It stands for an alternative view to those who discern sharp divides and interruptions of historical flows be it in 1945 or around 1990. The question is to what extent the Nordic cases fit the standard represented by Germany.

The Nordic Cases

The framework conditions in the Nordic countries differed not only from Germany but also from one another. Denmark and Norway were occupied by Germany, and the resistance myths in these two countries produced hegemonic meaning early after 1945. Finland between 1941 and 1944 fought the Soviet Union on the same side as Germany, so its war narrative contained a tension as to how close the military and political cooperation with Germany really was. Attempts were made to describe the relationship as independent, although Finland in the peace treaty of 1947 had to endorse the fact that the country had been in alliance with Germany. The war narrative underplayed the German role and emphasised the brave struggle against a superior enemy, a struggle that despite heavy losses made it possible to maintain Finnish independence. The geopolitical conditions of the Cold War set the limits for the degree to which Finland's circumvention of Germany could be articulated. Sweden escaped fighting the war, and developed after 1945 the neutrality myth which heroicised a skilful *realpolitische* manoeuvring that managed to prevent a German occupation. Iceland was occupied not by Germany but by Britain. The war has there played a much smaller role in the historiography and memory construction than full independence from Denmark did in June 1944, at about the same time as the Allies landed in Normandy. Icelandic historiography described a continuity from the nineteenth-century nationalistic fight for autonomy, in turn seen as stemming from the medieval saga period. This historiography had little room for Iceland's war experiences.

Despite such Nordic differences, each country displays patterns similar to those supporting the German model, although the confrontation between conflicting views on the past and the challenges of hegemonic narratives was weaker and more drawn-out. The historians and intellectuals in most countries – not only the Nordic region – want to identify their own *Historikerstreit*. It is 'in' to have had a confrontation about the past. However, 'confrontation' and '*Streit*' are elastic concepts. One swallow does not make a summer. Individual critical voices do not form a front line. They are not (yet) *geschichtsmässig*. Nothing comes close to the intensity of the German prototype. Moreover, the analogies often neglect the fact that in the German example, the attack in the 1980s came from the conservative historians.

In Denmark, the consensus on a story where almost the entire population resisted the occupation was challenged from the end of the 1970s until the 1990s by the second generation of post-war historians bent on using the term 'collaboration'. At the beginning of the twenty-first century, two generations after the war, a certain synthesis emerged between resistance and collaboration. In his chapter in this volume, Uffe Østergård refers to the shield-and-sword metaphor, which was used for the French self-understanding of the mix of Vichy collaboration and resistance. A self-understanding based on the idea of Denmark as a mini-France is an interesting thought, although maybe not without a certain hubris.

The challenge of the resistance narrative and the emphasis on collaboration was mainly driven by Denmark's professional historians. However, at about the same time as the synthetic view emerged among professional historians, collaboration was highlighted in a political campaign initiated by Prime Minister Anders Fogh Rasmussen of the centre-right coalition government, which was elected in 2001 and supported in parliament by the nationalist-populist People's Party. Politics took over memory construction. The wartime policy of accommodation was the target of the critique in a campaign that promoted the new government as a fresh start and a new moral state of mind. A political confrontation with the past would purify Denmark of old historical sins. The new morality was based on a self-understanding of Denmark as a champion of liberal values and tolerance. The political crusade had a much broader and deeper aim than the rewriting the past. It had, for instance, an obvious bearing on immigration politics. Foreigners who wanted to live in Denmark should be moulded after the Danish pattern. Islam was depicted as a new fundamentalist enemy. The vision of Denmark as the home of tolerance, embracing other Enlightenment values, was in terms of actual politics turned into intolerance. The Danish development has parallels to the Dutch situation. Is it just by chance that NATO in the era of the Iraq and Afghan wars has appointed general secretaries from these two countries, one of them indeed Anders Fogh Rasmussen? After the collapse of the Soviet system, NATO is looking for new meaning and new enemies. Moralism is replacing the *Realpolitik* of the Cold War. This is an era when the horizons of the early 1990s are narrowing. The open landscape created by the synthesis by the professional historians that Østergård refers to, seen in retrospect, after the beginning of the political campaign in 2001, was a synthesis reminding us of what Hegel said about Minerva's owl. While the historians published their synthesis, other and more influential voices were about to launch an alternative view of the past as an instrument for new politics for a new future. Moralism and confrontation, rather than synthesis and critical scepticism, became the carriers of history, the forces that were *geschichtsmässig*.

In Norway, as in Denmark, historians began to criticise the resistance myth in the 1970s. The resistance narrative was in particular developed by two leading historians with experience of the war and the resistance movement. Sverre Steen was the historical authority immediately after 1945, a member of the war investigation committee in 1945 and the editor of *Norges krig* ('Norway's war'). As a professor of history, he had been briefly arrested in the autumn of 1943. Magne Skodvin, an active member of the resistance movement, became a leading name in the historical research on the war following his Ph.D. thesis in 1956, *Striden om okkupasjonsstyret i Norge* ('The struggle over the occupation government in Norway').

The critique of Norway's resistance narrative gained increasing momentum in the 1980s and the 1990s. The focus shifted from the fighters in the resistance movements to the collaborators of various shapes, from Quisling and *Nasjonal Samling* to Norwegian women who had had sexual relations with German soldiers. One particular dispute among the historians dealt with David Irving's denial of the Holocaust. As in Denmark, the resistance narrative was developed in the 1950s and 1960s by historians with experience of the war years. A new generation of historians confronted the narrative in the 1970s and 1980s, but they remained critical voices in a discursive framework where 'resistance' continued to be the keyword, and where Quisling and the NS were seen as seducers of the Norwegian people, comparable to the Nazi criminals condemned in Nuremberg. The long-term relativisation of the resistance myth became more *geschichtsmässig* only in the 1990s after the end of the Cold War. Synne Corell's chapter in this volume shows that professional historians in Norway have had a stronger position in public debate, shaping the understanding of the past in a way that has offered less scope for, or interest in, massive political interventions such as the campaign by Fogh Rasmussen in Denmark. The negotiating of the past has had a more distinct academic cast in Norway.

This was less the case in Sweden. The heroicisation of adjustment, the translation of turncoat and time-server into key concepts such as 'small-state realism' and 'neutrality', held a paradigmatic position in post-war academic historiography and politics alike. As Johan Östling argues in his contribution in this volume, small-state realism could in retrospect be understood as small-state idealism, where Sweden was seen as a neutral and peaceful democracy intervening on the international scene. Only a limited number of contributions to the public debate challenged the master narrative, and it was much less historians who did this than voices in literature, film and theatre. There was a moralist subtext in this critique of the politics of continuous adjustment to international developments. What used to be labelled as cool and calculated neutrality now became a discourse about cowardly treachery. As in Norway, the critique never managed to become the carrier of a revised history until the 1990s, but *unlike* Norway, it was not a professional historian who triggered this development but a journalist. The academic experts followed up and cemented a new imagination of Sweden's post-war past. Self-righteousness gave way to self-criticism. A number of studies were published on anti-Semitism, racial biology, the Holocaust, and on collaboration with Nazi Germany during the Second World War and with the US during the Cold War. The policy of neutrality was relegated to the realm of hypocrisy.

In Finland, despite the formulations in the Paris Treaty about the Finnish–German alliance, the post-war narrative departed from the argument that Finland had pursued its own separate war against the Soviet Union, which had begun with a Soviet assault in November 1939. Gradually, Finland had slipped over to the German side. Finland was basically understood as a victim. Books by two American historians in 1957 and 1967 slowly imposed a more critical view on the origin of the war against the Soviet Union in 1941. The breakthrough of a more analytical/more nuanced view among Finnish historians came in the 1980s, thanks in no small measure to Soviet glasnost. However, another connected factor was the change of president in 1982 when Mauno Koivisto succeeded Urho Kekkonen. Unlike his predecessor Koivisto he did not see Finland in the shadow of the Soviet Union. Finland was no longer seen as driftwood, which the currents of time had washed onto the German side, but a boat skilfully steered into German waters. The new metaphor had clear similarities to the Swedish narrative on small-state realism. Henrik Meinander and other historians have in the 2000s confronted such revisionism, and emphasised the complexity in an existential war that was imposed upon Finland. They have done so in a broad public debate which has not only involved media and politics but has in fact been led by them.

The Nordic region demonstrates both similarities and differences compared to the German case. The Nordic cases have exhibited less of the German, almost Hegelian, confrontation of successive views on the past, representing more a gradual critique of their war myths from the 1970s onward. The critique has also tended to stick to one track and accelerated in the 1990s. In the Nordic countries, however, the role of academic historians has been less prominent than in Germany, diluted by voices from the media, politics and literature. The (extreme) Danish political campaign for a new history has in this respect been more pronounced than in the other Nordic countries (and in Germany). However, the absence of the historians from the initial destabilisation of the neutrality myth in Sweden is remarkable. The role of the academic historians has been most prominent in Norway, Denmark (until 2001) and Finland, although in Finland politics more than in the rest of the Nordic region has formulated the problem.

A European Pattern of Memory Construction?

What of other European patterns of coming to terms with the past? In France, wartime resistance informed the foundation myth of the Fourth Republic (1946–1958). The favourite metaphor of the older generation of historians was the shield and the sword, where Vichy was the shield and De Gaulle the sword. The shield myth held that Vichy was necessary to protect the French from even worse excesses at the hands of a purely German administration. The regime under Field Marshal Pétain acted primarily beneficially, shielding France. De Gaulle's incarnation as the sword refers to his book in 1932, *Le fil de l'épée* ('The edge of the sword'), where he wrote of military leadership.

As in Germany and the Nordic countries, French critique of the resistance narrative emerged in the 1970s, although, similar to

Finland, it was initiated by an American historian. In 1972, Robert Paxton published *Vichy France: Old Guard New Order*, where he argued that the German authorities were primarily indifferent and impassive to the French authorities and the prospect of collaboration. Direct interference in the Vichy administration from Berlin was almost non-existent. The German General Staff were unwilling to consider the overtures in 1941 for greater French independence in return for more assistance for Germany.[14] This glossing over of the role of the Vichy regime reinforced the shield metaphor.

The critique from within France began in the 1970s with a focus on France and anti-Semitism. However, it gained momentum and became *geschichtsmässig* only at the end of the 1980s. In 1987, Henry Rousso published *Le syndrome de Vichy de 1944 à nos jours*, with the aim of challenging and crushing the national myth based on *la Résistance*.[15] He coined the phrase the '*passé qui ne passe pas*' ('the past that does not pass'). The expression was possibly inspired by Ernst Nolte's article of 6 June 1986, entitled 'Die Vergangenheit, die nicht vergehen will' in the prelude to the German *Historikerstreit*. Rousso explained the influence of the complicated domestic political conflicts during the occupation on the public debate ever since 1945. He argued that the French were obsessed by the past, victims of the 'religion of memory', taking the term syndrome from psychoanalytical theory. The traumas of the Vichy period remained in the collective consciousness, transmitted as in a neurosis from incompleted mourning to repression and finally to an obsessive fixation on the trauma. Rousso demonstrated how French re-unification and modernisation in the 1950s and 1960s were based on political myths about De Gaulle's unifying role and a strong resistance movement but how this image was crushed in the 1970s by a debate weighed down by guilt for anti-Semitism and the responsibility of the French people for the Holocaust. In order to liberate France from the trauma that Vichy represented, Rousso recommended public debate. He had his request granted, and in 1994 he came back with a new book, *Vichy: Un passé qui ne passe pas*. Co-written with the journalist Eric Conan, he now recommended not a public debate but a moratorium. According to Rousso and Conan, if 'one is not allowed to forget', one is ultimately unable to confront the present and the future. The old myth was broken, but a new was about to take form about collaboration and guilt. Rousso and Conan argued that the problem with this development was that historians had been pushed aside by journalists, who were better at producing hysteria than historical understanding.[16]

There are in this French memory and myth construction parallels to the growing critique of the official re-foundation myths after 1945 in Germany and the Nordic countries. The reassessment slowly undermined the credibility of the established stories, so slowly in fact that it was only in the 1980s and 1990s that it gained the capacity to serve as a carrier of a new historical outline. One striking difference in the French debate is the connection to psychoanalytical theories, which surfaced later in Germany, under French influence, but much less so in the Nordic countries.[17]

In Italy, historians after the war constructed a past in which the members of the resistance movement became the heroes, while evil emanated from the German occupation forces. The paradoxical consequence of this foundation myth, which was written from the perspective of the political Left, was that the role of domestic Fascism was played down and Italian war history became as heroic as that of the French, the Dutch, the Danish, the Norwegian and all others that had had a resistance movement. Minimising the role of Fascism in Italy was, on the whole, an unintentional consequence rather than the outcome of a conscious decision, brought about by an overwhelming focus on the resistance. The analysis of Fascism depicted a well-demarcated reactionary movement and, subsequently, a regime that, by means of violence, terror and surveillance, suppressed the democratic and progressive Italian nation. In this respect, there was an obvious similarity between the mythology of the Federal Republic of Germany in the 1950s and the development of the myth in Italy by Liberals, Christian Democrats, Socialists, and Communists up to the 1970s.

This foundation myth was questioned in the 1960s by the conservative historian Renzo De Felice.[18] In the first volume of his biography of Mussolini, published in 1965, he gave serious consideration to the revolutionary socialist stance Mussolini had adopted prior to 1915. He used this as a point of departure in problematising the antagonism between Fascism and Communism/Socialism, which is one of the key elements in the myth of the *resistenza*. De Felice then continued step by step in his undertaking to demolish the myth. In the volumes on *Mussolini il duce* (1974 and 1981), he argued that there had been a basic consensus between the leader and people and that the *resistenza* had no popular backing until the fortunes of war turned. In his last, triple volume (1990–1997), he was very explicit in his interrogation of the resistance movement, both as history and as a foundation myth.[19] When he first launched his attack on the myth, De Felice was widely regarded as a maverick, but gradually his view came to be highly important in research on Fascism. His campaign against the foundation myth should, however, be seen in a broader political framework, beyond the professional debate among historians. De Felice's work was an element of a wider campaign against the Communist Party that took place in the 1970s. There are interesting parallels here to Nolte's campaign in Germany that triggered the German *Historikerstreit*. However, the difference is that there was no German-style *Historikerstreit* in Italy. The debate was much less spectacular and much less of a hot public topic.

The Italian debate on how to come to terms with the past is now moving in the direction of synthesis, where emphasis is given to the plurality of memories. The Left, the Right and the Catholic world all have their views on the role of anti-Fascism in developing the post-war republican *credo*. The revisionism initiated by De Felice in the struggle over memory has produced a synthetical response.[20]

The Nordic countries in the European memory construction

To compare the memory construction around the Second World War in the Nordic countries with its European counterparts entails the comparison of diversity with an even bigger diversity. The differences between the Nordic countries are obvious from the contributions to this volume. Different historical settings and experiences have produced different histories. European diversity is, of course, an order of greater magnitude. The cases presented here should just be seen as examples, nothing more, nothing less.

Despite the Nordic and European diversity in terms of re-foundation myths and memory construction, there are some recurring patterns. One observation is that critical challenges to the heroic narratives began in the 1970s, led by professional historians or, as in Sweden, by media and literary figures. However, the critique only slowly eroded the master narratives. It was in the 1990s that the critique found broader societal support, which then brought the old narratives to collapse. What arose in their place were new, more-or-less moralistic accounts of collaboration instead of resistance, veiled cooperation instead of neutrality. In the Swedish case, the critique developed a continuity between the Second World War and the Cold War. In the other Nordic countries, the critique was more focused on the Second World War itself. The wider support made the critique *geschichtsmässig*, carrying an alternative historical narrative in all the Nordic countries.

The emerging master narrative after 1990 was built on imaginations of universal values in the name of enlightened liberalism. In the 2000s, the moralist tendency in the language of tolerance gave it a twist of intolerance in its demarcation of that which was said not to be tolerant and not to belong to the West, in particular Islam. The process of demarcation and 'otherisation' let nationalism and populism return. The end of the Cold War had left a gap where its mobilising discourses based on dichotomies of friend–enemy and white–black were missing. Ten years after 1990, the gap was about to be filled by an Islamic enemy.

The nation has been the locus of the propagation of universal and transnational values. The rhetoric about universalism and transnational, global exchange and the flow of ideas, goods and capital emerged in many national versions. Despite the pretensions in concepts such as 'universal' and 'transnational' they have not really managed to transcend their national settings.

There was certainly a critical and moralist confrontation with idealised and heroic national pasts around 1990, but translated into a European future this confrontation was naïve. Borrowing from Francis Fukuyama's fantasies about the end of history, a unified Europe that had overcome the historical East–West divide was proclaimed. The triumph of liberalism in 1989 – and the rhetoric of the globalisation narrative that followed in its wake – implied the ideological unification not only of Europe but of the whole world. Such illusions ended with the civil wars in Yugoslavia and the onset of a new religious war viewed as a 'clash of civilisations'.[21]

The moral dimension to the foundation myths and the critique of those myths means moralism was a constant. The continuity is evident if one turns to Reinhart Koselleck and the term 'hypocrisy' in his argument that history is written by the winners. He develops his argument through the sequence of critique–crisis–hypocrisy with reference to the fact that the Greek terms crisis and hypocrisy have the same etymological origin.[22]

In the past ten to fifteen years, references to the past have increasingly been made in terms of memory rather than history. There is a connection between history and memory, of course, but what is it, and why the shift? 'Memory' has come to be understood in many different ways. An elastic concept, it has lost meaning in proportion to its growing rhetorical power.[23] The most common reasons for developing a usable past are linked to individual and collective identity claims. A sense of sameness over time and space is sustained by remembering. There is little overall coherence in 'collective memory' studies, but probably the most important dividing line is that between individual and collective memory.[24]

The term memory means that the constructivist approach is emphasised far more than in conventional history. This difference, in turn, is based on the growing insight that history is much less about discovering a deserted past waiting for explorers than it is about constructing a past that gives meaning to the present and helps us to imagine the future.

The conceptual slide from history to memory clearly relates to the construction of legitimacy. Who are the analysts of the past whose statements produce social cohesion and political legitimacy? During the nineteenth century, historians were key actors in the construction of foundation mythologies and the building of the nation-state. What role do professional historians play in this process today, and what degree of exclusivity do they have? Less than their predecessors, one would argue. One decisive difference between then and now is the epistemological shift from a belief that historians, by means of analysis of the sources, were discovering the past as it was, to the belief today that history is about the construction of one possible past among other conceivable pasts, and that the narrative is as much about the present as about the past.

The dramatic events around 1990 provoked a search for the historical roots of a turbulent present. The Cold War no longer fulfilled the role as an interpretative framework. The revision of the past in order to understand better both present developments and future prospects resulted in what can be described as a 'memory boom'. At the time of this memory boom, when the past not only has been recognised as a subject of scholarly research but has also been widely employed and represented in politics and the mass media, it is more useful to speak of different discourses of the past than to recall again the distinction between history and memory. These different types of discourse – academic, political-institutional, popular or everyday, media, etc. – are not easily separable, as they intermingle and influence one another.

The questions remain, however. Do professional historians possess an exclusive capacity for dealing with the past? And what is their role vis-à-vis the use of history as entertainment, as political legitimisation or as the subject of non-professional inquiry? The cultural turn in the 1980s and the emergence of constructivist methodologies have resulted in the view that historians do not stand above the processes that they analyse. Rather, they are considered to be part of them, and their position as interpreters of the past has thus been relativised. In the wake of Foucault's work, it is not only history but also epistemological schemes in general that are deemed ideological and largely political. The past is hence constantly present in the present.

Such epistemological developments and the search for new theoretical structures after the end of the Cold War have made the role of professional historians less exclusive. Politicians and media representatives participate more actively in the remaking of the past, which is a crucial dimension in the conceptual slide from history to memory. This democratising dimension of the new conceptualisation, with less exclusivity (and authority) for professional historians, is counter-balanced by a populist dimension that runs the risk of manipulation and abuse – rather than use – of history. Another growing trend conflates history with a nostalgic interest in the past that lacks theoretical framing. This trend could be called history as *kitsch.*

The new conceptual and symbolic topography affecting concepts such as identity and memory must be understood in the light of experiences of intellectual disorientation and of the erosion, since the 1970s, of earlier, established frameworks of interpretation. A result of fundamental changes in epistemology, technology and the organisation of economies, work and labour markets, these shifts have produced new views, both of the past and of the preconditions for history – the science of the past. History as 'science' is a translation of the German *Wissenschaft.* Since the nineteenth century, the writing of the past has been seen in Germany as analogous to the description of nature, or *Naturwissenschaften.* In English-speaking cultures, history was never categorised as a science, but was part of the realm of the arts. This distinction between the two linguistic cultures, so long ignored, has recently begun to take on meaning. The writing of history is perhaps less a matter of the unproblematic discovery of a past 'out there' by means of refined techniques of source criticism, like establishing causative relationships in a laboratory. It rather depends on the context of the present where the narrative is composed. This insight is as important as the facts on which the narrative is based. The recognition of the role of narration poses new problems along the science–art axis.[25]

The cases of the Nordic countries, Germany, France and Italy all illustrate that history in the form of foundation myth is not a given, set in stone once and for all. On the contrary, this history is continuously reconsidered and renegotiated, and in this ongoing process some periods appear to be characterised by greater transformation than others. Master narratives are repeatedly challenged by counter narratives. However, at some historical junctures the master narratives take on hegemonic features while at others they collapse and lose their capacity to convince. These junctures are the points where established facts and events, the building blocks of the narratives about the past, rapidly lose their strength as carriers of history, their *Geschichtsmässigkeit,* and give way to new carriers of the imaginations of the past.

Notes

1 The argument is developed in Małgorzata Pakier & Bo Stråth, 'Introduction: A European Memory?', in: Małgorzata Pakier & Bo Stråth (eds.), *A European Memory? Contested Histories and Politics of Remembrance* (Oxford, 2010).

2 Francis Fukuyama, *The End of History and the Last Man* (New York, 1992).

3 It is difficult to find a good translation for the term *Geschichtsmässig*. Literally, the term refers to history or 'carrier of history'. For some reason, some facts and events are ignored in historical narratives while others become constitutive parts of them. For the term *Geschichtsmässig*, see Wolfgang Schmale, *Scheitert Europa an seinem Mythendefizit?* (Bochum, 1997). For foundation myths and the connections between history, myth and memory, see Bo Stråth (ed.), *Myth and Memory in the Construction of Community: Historical Patterns in Europe and Beyond* (Brussels, 2000). For a general discussion of historians, foundation myths and the Second World War, see Richard J.B. Bosworth, *Explaining Auschwitz and Hiroshima: Historians and the Second World War 1945–1990* (London, 1993).

4 Bo Stråth, 'Introduction. Myth, Memory and History in the Construction of Community', in: Bo Stråth (ed.), *Myth and Memory in the Construction of Community: Historical Patterns in Europe and Beyond* (Brussels, 2000).

5 For the construction of collective memories – only individuals have memories, while collective memory is a social construct – see Pakier & Stråth 2010.

6 In 1965, the East German historian Ernst Engelberg stated: 'Both liberalism and Jacobin radicalism showed from the very beginning and show it time and again that democracy and dictatorship are not contradictions. One always has to ask the question: Democracy for whom? Dictatorship against whom? [...] in reality, parliamentary bourgeois democracy is, on the one hand, a means to tune in the interests of the different parties of the urban and rural capitalists to each other; on the other hand, a means to press down the workers and the other labourers.'

Such an understanding of democracy, as the Dutch historian Jan Herman Brinks has argued, bore strong similarities to the concept of democracy as it was articulated by the 'conservative revolutionary' Carl Schmitt, who was one of the trailblazers of the Third Reich. As a matter of fact, 'anti-Fascism' in the GDR represented the failure to purge the state and the *Sozialistische Einheitspartei Deutschlands* SED adequately of Nazi followers. West German authors as well as Simon Wiesenthal have observed that some former Nazis were allowed to find their way back into political life in the GDR. The historian Ernst Engelberg would later write his great biography of Bismarck. See Jan Herman Brinks, *Die DDR-Geschichtswissenschaft auf dem Weg zur deutschen Einheit: Luther, Friedrich II und Bismarck als Paradigmen politischen Wandels* (Frankfurt am Main, 1992).

7 Bernhard Giesen, *Intellectuals and the German Nation: Collective Memory in an Axial Age* (Cambridge, 1998).

8 Victor Klemperer, *Ich will Zeugniss ablegen bis zum letzten: Tagebücher* (Berlin, 1995); and Victor Klemperer, *So sitze ich denn zwischen allen Stühlen: Tagebücher 1945–1959*, 2 vols. (Berlin, 1999).

9 Fritz Fischer, *Griff nach der Weltmacht: Die Kriegspolitik des kaiserlichen Deutschlands, 1914–1918* (Düsseldorf, 1961).
10 Ernst Nolte, *Der europäische Bürgerkrieg 1917–1945: Nationalsozialismus und Bolchewismus* (Berlin, 1987).
11 Hans-Ulrich Wehler, *Aus der Geschichte lernen?* (Munich, 1988).
12 Jürgen Kocka (ed.), *Bürgertum im 19. Jahrhundert: Deutschland im europäischen Vergleich* (Munich, 1988).
13 Günter Grass, *Im Krebsgang: Eine Novelle* (Munich, 2009). For the Allied bombings, see Jörg Friedrich, *Der Brand: Deutschland im Bombenkrieg 1940–1945* (Berlin, 2002); Jörg Friedrich, *Brandstätten: Der Anblick des Bombenkriegs* (Berlin, 2003); Anthony C. Grayling, *Die toten Städte* (Munich, 2007).
14 Robert O. Paxton, *Vichy France: Old Guard New Order* (New York, 1972).
15 Henry Rousso, *Le syndrome de Vichy de 1944 à nos jours* (Paris, 1987).
16 Henry Rousso & Eric Conan, *Vichy: Un passé qui ne passé pas* (Paris, 1994).
17 For the psychoanalytical influence on the German debate, see Giesen 1998 and Bernhard Giesen, 'National Identity as Trauma: the German Case', in: Bo Stråth (ed.), *Myth and Memory in the Construction of Community. Historical Patterns in Europe and Beyond* (Brussels, 2000).
18 Renzo De Felice, *Mussolino il rivoluzionario, 1883–1920* (Turin, 1976); Renzo De Felice, *Mussolino il fascista* (Turin, 1976).
19 Renzo De Felice, *Mussolini il Duce* (Turin, 1974); De Felice 1976; and Renzo De Felice, *Mussolino: L'alleato*, 2 vols. (Turin, 1990–1997); cf. Claudio Pavone, *Una Guerra civile: Saggio storico sulla moralità nella Resistenza* (Turin, 1991).
20 See Leonardo Paggi, *Le Memorie della Repubblica* (Florence, 1999).
21 Samuel Huntington, *The Clash of Civilizations and the Remaking of World Order* (New York, 1996).
22 Reinhart Koselleck, *Kritik und Krise: Eine Studie zur Pathogenese der bürgerlichen Welt* (Freiburg, 1959); cf. Hagen Schulz-Forberg & Bo Stråth, *The Political History of European Integration: The Hypocrisy of Democracy-through-Market* (London, 2010).
23 John Gillis (ed.), *Commemorations: The Politics of National Identity* (Princeton, NJ, 1994), 3.
24 James Wertsch, *Voices of Collective Remembering* (Cambridge, 2002), 34–35.
25 Stråth 2000.

Contributors

Synne Corell received her Ph.D. at the University of Oslo in 2010 with a dissertation on the Norwegian historiography of the German occupation of Norway during the Second World War, *Krigens ettertid: Okkupasjonshistorien i norske historiebøker* (Scandinavian Academic Press, 2011). Her current interests include the relationship between memory and history, and the history, of minorities in and migration to Norway with particular focus on Jewish history.

Guðmundur Hálfdanarson is Professor of History at the University of Iceland, specializing in European social and political history. He was educated at Lund University, the University of Iceland and Cornell University. Among his most recent publications are *Íslenska þjóðríkið – upphaf og endimörk* ('The Icelandic Nation State – Origins and Limits') (2001); (with H. Jensen and L. Berntson) *Europa 1800–2000* (2003); *Historical Dictionary of Iceland* (2nd edn, 2008); and *Discrimination and Tolerance in European Perspective* (editor, 2008). He is the editor-in-chief of the *Scandinavian Journal of History*.

Henrik Meinander is Professor of History at the University of Helsinki. His main publications have focused on Finnish and North European twentieth-century history, especially on the societal and cultural aspects of war, sport, education and historiography. His best-known work is probably *A History of Finland* (an edition in English has recently been published by Hurst & Co.). Meinander is currently leading a research project funded by the Academy of Finland on 'Wartime emotions: A cultural history of Finland, 1939–1951'.

Mirja Österberg is a Ph.D. student in history at the Centre for Nordic Studies at the University of Helsinki. She is working on a dissertation about Finnish Social Democrats in the 1930s and 1940s and how the Nordic cooperation they were drawn into influenced their socio-political argumentation.

Uffe Østergård is Professor in European and Danish History at the International Center for Business and Politics, Copenhagen Business School having been Jean Monnet professor in European civilization, University of Aarhus, and director of the Danish Center for Holocaust and Genocide Studies at the Danish Institute International Studies, Copenhagen. His research interests are: Danish historiography, history and political culture; modern European history; the First and Second World Wars; comparative studies of Nazism and Fascism; national identity, nationalism and nation-branding; European civilization and integration; and the Holocaust in European history.

Johan Östling is a Postdoctoral Research Fellow at the Department of History, Lund University. He has written extensively on modern Swedish and German history, National Socialism and narratives of the Second World War, historiography, and history culture. His dissertation, *Nazismens sensmoral: Svenska erfarenheter i andra världskrigets efterdyning* (2008), was awarded several prizes, including the Clio Prize and the Nils Klim Prize. Östling is currently working on a project on the transformation of the Humboldtian tradition and the idea of the university in twentieth-century Germany.

Henrik Stenius is Research Director of the Centre for Nordic Studies at the University of Helsinki. He has previously been acting professor at the Department of History at Helsinki University and Director of the Finnish Institute in London. His fields of research are the history of mobilization and voluntary associations in the Nordic countries, and conceptual history. He is a member of the Finnish Centre of Excellence of Political Thought and Conceptual Change and the Nordic Centre of Excellence of Nordic Welfare Research.

Bo Stråth is Academy of Finland Distinguished Professor in Nordic, European and World History at Helsinki University. In 1997–2007 he was professor of contemporary history at the European University Institute, Florence, and 1990–1996 professor of history at the

University of Gothenburg. In his current research he is concentrating on two major projects, 'Between Restoration and Revolution, National Constitutions and Global Law', co-directed with Martti Koskenniemi, and 'Conceptual History and Global Translations'. He has published extensively on European modernity and European integration.